Teaching Economics

Using Children's Literature

D1310901

Written by

Harlan R. Day, Ph.D.
Indiana Department of Education

Johnetta Dolon
Delaware Community School Corporation

MaryAnn Foltz
Delaware Community School Corporation

Kathy Heyse
Concord Community Schools

Callie Marksbary
Lafayette School Corporation

Mary Sturgeon
Lafayette School Corporation

INDIANA DEPARTMENT OF EDUCATION
Center for School Improvement and Performance
Office of Program Development
September 1997

Revised 2006

Original Acknowledgements

Some of the clip art in this curriculum is from the following publications of the Carson-Dellosa Publishing Company, Inc: Clip Art Collection I, Clip Art Collection II, and Kids' Clip Art. Permission granted.

The Indiana Department of Education (IDOE) thanks the National Council on Economic Education for permission to use annotated bibliographic entries from several of its excellent publications.

Generous financial support for this curriculum project was provided by the **Economics**America program of the Indiana Council for Economic Education (ICEE). **Nancy Vollmer** and **Andria Duke** of the ICEE staff also helped compile the annotated bibliography, as did **Betty Sue Williams**, classroom teacher from Centerville Elementary in Oldham County, Kentucky.

A special thanks is extended to **David Ballard**, Economic Education Consultant with IDOE, and to **Susan Bougher** and **Jennifer Banning**, teachers at Miller School in the Lafayette School Corporation, for their creative ideas and support of this project.

The authors are also grateful to the publication staff of IDOE for their excellent layout and art work and to **Jayne Hershman** of West Lafayette, Indiana, who edited the final version of this curriculum.

Current Acknowledgements

The Indiana Department of Education (IDOE) is grateful to the dedicated teacher-authors who spent so much time developing the lessons for this and the original edition. IDOE also thanks the **Indiana Council for Economic Education (ICEE)** for its diligent work in leading the revision efforts. ICEE secretaries, **Nancy Vollmer** and **Shelly Surber**, were a great help in formatting the document.

Funding for this revision of *Teaching Economics Using Children's Literature* was provided by the **National Council on Economic Education (NCEE)**. *Teaching Economics Using Children's Literature* is distributed exclusively by the NCEE.

National Council on Economic Education
1140 Avenue of the Americas
New York, NY 10036
Phone: 212.730.7007 or 1.800.338.1192
www.ncee.net
Email: sales@ncee.net

Table of Contents

Teaching Economics Using Children's Literature
Correlation with the National Standards for Economics*

Standards/Lessons	1	2	3	4	5	6	7	8	9	10	11
1. Scarcity		✔	✔				✔				
• Goods & Services	✔	✔		✔		✔		✔	✔		✔
• Producers						✔			✔	✔	
• Consumers										✔	
• Productive Resources	✔	✔	✔	✔		✔		✔		✔	
• Opportunity Cost							✔	✔			✔
• Trade-offs											
2. Marginal costs/ marginal benefits											
3. Allocation of goods and services											
4. Role of incentives											
5. Gain from trade											
6. Specialization and trade	✔				✔	✔		✔	✔	✔	
• Interdependence					✔	✔				✔	
7. Markets – price and quantity determination		✔	✔							✔	
8. Role of price in market system										✔	
9. Role of competition											
10. Role of economic institutions											
• Savings								✔			✔
• Investing								✔			
11. Role of money											
12. Role of interest rates											
13. Role of resources in determining income											
14. Profit and the entrepreneur				✔							
15. Growth											
16. Role of government									✔		
17. Using cost/benefit analysis to evaluate government pgms											
18. Macroeconomy – income/employment, prices											
19. Unemployment and inflation											
20. Monetary and fiscal policy											

* Voluntary National Content Standards in Economics, National Council on Economic Education (NCEE), 1997.

Teaching Economics Using Children's Literature
Correlation with the National Standards for Economics*

12	13	14	15	16	17	18	19	20	21	22	23	24
		✔	✔	✔	✔	✔	✔	✔		✔	✔	✔
✔					✔							
✔		✔									✔	✔
✔		✔									✔	
✔	✔	✔		✔		✔	✔	✔	✔	✔		✔
		✔			✔	✔	✔	✔	✔			✔
				✔								
						✔				✔		
						✔	✔			✔		✔
	✔					✔						
✔			✔		✔			✔			✔	
			✔		✔						✔	
										✔		
	✔	✔								✔		
	✔								✔			
									✔			
			✔					✔	✔			
							✔				✔	✔
			✔		✔							

* Voluntary National Content Standards in Economics, National Council on Economic Education (NCEE), 1997.

Introduction

There is a growing recognition from educators and other opinion leaders that to be effective citizens, students must have a basic understanding of the economic world around them. Many excellent curriculum materials have been developed recently to help accomplish this important task. This new elementary curriculum booklet, *Teaching Economics Using Children's Literature*, is another addition to the growing collection of materials. The booklet contains practical, classroom-tested lessons to use with popular children's stories. The economic concepts used in this curriculum are identified in *Indiana's Academic Standards — Social Studies* and the *Voluntary National Content Standards* developed by the National Council on Economic Education.

Why Use Children's Literature?

Why is using children's literature to teach economics so effective? First, since children (and teachers!) love stories, using literature is a very motivational teaching technique. Second, as economic concepts are taught within the context of literature, students realize that economics is a very real and interesting part of the world around them. And third, using children's literature allows teachers, as the proverb says, "to kill two birds with one stone." In a crowded curriculum, this interdisciplinary approach is certainly appealing and may even be necessary.

Using the Curriculum

The main part of *Teaching Economics Using Children's Literature* consists of 24 lessons, each providing ideas and teaching activities to accompany a specific story or book. In Part 3, the curriculum contains "generic" handouts that can be used with any children's book. These handouts include two very useful decision models: the Decision Tree (from the popular *Econ and Me* video series) and the Five-Step Decision Grid. Finally, Part 5 is a Literature Connection section that identifies many other books that can be used to teach economics. These books — and short lessons on each one — can be found at the popular KidsEcon Posters© web site. (www.kidseconposters.com — Click on Literature Connection.)

Additional Lessons: The original edition of *Teaching Economics Using Children's Literature* contained lessons on these five books, which are no longer in print: *The Little Painter of Sabana Grande, All the Money in the World, Cally's Enterprise, Kid Power Strikes Back,* and *Leave the Cooking to Me.* Teachers may download these original lessons at **www.econed-in.org/programs.asp**.

A Key Assumption

Teaching Economics Using Children's Literature is based on the key assumption that teachers already have a basic understanding of the economic concepts presented in the lessons. For example, individual lessons contain no detailed explanations of economic concepts nor are answers provided to simple questions on the handouts. However, Part 1 of this curriculum does contain definitions and explanations of 25 basic economic concepts — in regular and student language. These definitions will be a great help to teachers who want to update their knowledge of economics.

The Indiana Department of Education is confident that you will enjoy using these lessons to make economics come alive for your students through the exciting world of children's literature.

For More Information

For further information about curriculum materials or training in economics education, please contact the **Indiana Department of Education**, Office of Program Development, Room 229, State House, Indianapolis, IN 46204-2798, (317) 232-9186. Indiana teachers may also contact the **Indiana Council for Economic Education**. (www.econed-in.org)

Teachers in other states should contact the Councils or Centers for Economic Education in the affiliated network of the **National Council on Economic Education**. See www.ncee.net.

Part 1

Economic Concepts

This section describes the economic concepts identified throughout this curriculum booklet. They are described in regular and student language.

Goods	Trade-Offs
Services	Money
Consumers	Price
Producers	Marketplace
Productive Resources	Exchange and Trade
Natural Resources	Specialization
Human Resources	Interdependence
Capital Resources	Productivity
Entrepreneur	Economic Systems
Production Model	Profit
Scarcity	Role of Government
Opportunity Cost	International Trade
	Circular Flow Model

These definitions and explanations are based on the *Voluntary National Content Standards,* developed by the National Council on Economic Education (NCEE), *A Framework for Teaching Basic Economic Concepts* (NCEE), *Economics: What and When* (NCEE), and *Indiana's Academic Standards — Social Studies.*

Goods

Content Statement: Goods are tangible items that people want.

Student Language: A good is something people want that they can touch and hold.

Example: Any item you can buy at a store is a good.

Services

Content Statement: Services are activities that satisfy people's wants.

Student Language: A service is something that one person does for someone else.

Example: Washing a car, fixing a lawn mower, cutting hair, or teaching students are examples of services.

Consumers

Content Statement: Consumers are people who satisfy their wants by using goods and services.

Student Language: Consumers are people who buy goods and services.

Example: When Sarah purchased a dress, she was a consumer.

Producers

Content Statement: Producers combine productive resources to make goods and provide services.

Student Language: Producers are people who make goods and provide services.

Example: A mechanic is a producer of car repair services.

Productive Resources

Content Statement: Productive resources are all natural, human, and capital resources used in the production of goods and services.

Student Language: Productive resources are the natural, human, and capital resources we need to produce goods and services.

Example: Steel, plastic, different types of workers, and many kinds of tools and equipment are some of the productive resources necessary to produce a car.

Natural Resources

Content Statement: Natural resources (often collectively referred to as "land") are the "gifts of nature" necessary for production. They are present without human intervention.

Student Language: Natural resources are things found in nature that we use in production.

Example: Oil, water, air, minerals, wild animals, and land are examples of natural resources.

Attention! Strictly speaking, natural resources refer only to items found naturally without any human intervention. Thus, any raw materials that have been to some degree processed by humans, such as the cotton cloth or metal zippers used to make blue jeans, are technically not natural resources. However, with elementary students it is helpful to include the raw materials of production under the category of natural resources.

Human Resources

Content Statement: Human resources, also called labor, represent the quantity and quality of human effort used in production.

Student Language: Human resources are the people who work in jobs to produce goods and services.

Example: Line workers, secretaries, managers, and engineers are examples of the human resources used to produce an automobile.

Attention!   The special skills that workers acquire through education and training are referred to as *human capital*. It takes time and resources to acquire human capital. Workers who have accumulated human capital are usually paid more than those who haven't because they are likely to be more productive.

Capital Resources

Content Statement: Capital resources are goods that are produced and used to make *other* goods and services.

Student Language: Capital resources are special goods such as tools, equipment, machines, and buildings which are used to produce other goods and services.

Example: The school building and all the equipment in it are capital resources needed to produce education.

Attention!   Wild animals are properly classified as natural resources. But animals used to help in production, such as plow animals, should be considered capital resources.

Entrepreneur

Content Statement: Entrepreneurs are people who organize other productive resources to make goods and services. They assume the risk of economic lose and gain profits if they are successful.

Student Language: Entrepreneurs are people who take the risk to start a business. They have to organize all of the productive resources to produce goods and services.

Example: Henry Ford was an entrepreneur who used his personal savings to design a factory which produced automobiles on an assembly line.

Production Model

Content Statement: The production model illustrates how the three productive resources are combined to produce goods and services.

Student Language: The production model shows how the three productive resources are combined to produce goods and services.

Example:

Production

Productive Resources

Natural Resources		Human Resources		Capital Resources		
	+		+		→	Goods and Services
		Inputs				**Output**

Scarcity

Content Statement:

Scarcity is the condition of not being able to have all of the goods and services that one wants. It exists because there are not enough productive resources to produce all that people want. Because of scarcity, people must make choices.

Student Language:

Scarcity means not being able to have everything that we want. Scarcity forces us to make choices.

Example:

When you go shopping, your limited income forces you to make choices. You can't buy everything you want!

Attention!

In certain situations, a good may not seem scarce. For example, you may have too many desks in your classroom and want to get rid of some. In an economic sense, however, a desk is still a scarce good. It has a price, is not freely available, and the resources that were used to produce a desk had an alternative use.

Opportunity Cost

Content Statement:

The opportunity cost of a choice is the value of the best alternative given up.

Student Language:

When you make a decision, the most valuable alternative that you *don't* choose is your opportunity cost.

Example:

Sue wants to be a nurse and teacher, but she can't be both. She decides to be a nurse, so being a teacher is her opportunity cost.

Attention!

Your opportunity cost is *not* the sum of all possible alternatives. Suppose Sue also wants to be a secretary, but it is her third choice. Her opportunity cost — being a teacher — would not change by choosing to be a nurse. Your opportunity cost is the best alternative forgone when making a choice.

Trade-Offs

Content Statement:	Trade-Offs means getting a little more of one option in exchange for a little less of something else. Few choices are all-or-nothing decisions; most involve trade-offs.
Student Language:	Trade-offs means getting a little less of one thing in order to get a little more of another.
Example:	Jeff loved to buy baseball cards. So when he used part of his birthday money to buy some candy instead, he was trading off cards for candy.

Money

Content Statement:	Money is anything commonly used to exchange goods and services. To be effective, money must be scarce, durable, portable, and divisible.
Student Language:	Money is what people use to buy goods and services.
Example:	Many different items have been used as money throughout history, including gold, silver, shells, tobacco, and paper.

Price

Content Statement:	The price is what people pay when they buy a good or service and what they receive when they sell a good or service. In a free market, price is determined by supply and demand.
Student Language:	The price is the amount of money that people pay when they buy a good or service. It is determined by the buying and selling decisions of consumers and producers.
Example:	Sue paid a price of $ .50 for the pack of gum.
Attention!	Prices change constantly, depending on changes in supply and demand. At the *market clearing price,* the amount buyers want to buy equals the amount sellers want to sell.

Marketplace (Market)

Content Statement: A marketplace, or market, exists whenever buyers and sellers exchange goods and services.

Student Language: Markets are places where people buy and sell goods and services.

Example: At the farmer's market, I purchased some apples.

Exchange and Trade

Content Statement: Exchange is the trading of goods and services for other goods and services or for money. Barter is trading without money. People exchange goods and services because they expect to be better off after the exchange.

Student Language: Exchange is the trading of goods and services for money or for other goods and services. Barter is trading without money. People exchange goods and services because they expect to be better off after the exchange.

Example: When John went to the store, he exchanged $15 for a soccer ball. Roberto bartered his used bat for Jerry's kickball.

Specialization

Content Statement:	People specialize when they produce a narrower range of goods and services than they consume. Specialization increases productivity and results in greater interdependence.
Student Language:	People specialize when they work in jobs where they produce a few special goods and services. When people specialize, they produce more but they also depend more on one another.
Example:	John is a mechanic. He gets his hair cut at Joe's Barber Shop. Joe goes to John to get his car fixed. John and Joe earn more by specializing, but they must depend on one another.
Attention! 	*Division of labor* is a "special" kind of specialization. It occurs when the production of a good is broken down into numerous separate tasks, with different workers performing each task. It differs from *unit production*, where individual workers produce an entire product.

Interdependence

Content Statement:	Interdependence occurs when people and nations depend on one another to provide for each other's wants. Greater specialization and trade lead to greater interdependence.
Student Language:	Interdependence occurs when people and nations depend on one another to provide the goods and services they want. The more people specialize and trade, the more interdependent they become.
Example:	Canada and the United States are very interdependent because they trade so much with one another.

Productivity

Content Statement:	Productivity is a ratio of output (goods and services) produced per unit of input (productive resources) over some period of time.
Student Language:	Productivity measures how many goods and services are produced over a period of time. It is usually measured as output per hour. You can increase productivity by producing more goods and services with the same resources or by producing the same goods and services with fewer resources.
Example:	When Mary purchased a snowblower she greatly increased her productivity — she was able to clean many more sidewalks each day.

Economic Systems

Content Statement:	Every society has an economic system, the institutional framework a society uses to allocate its productive resources to produce and distribute goods and services. An economic system answers these questions: 1. *What* goods and services will be produced? 2. *How* will goods and services be produced? 3. *Who* will consume the goods and services? The three fundamental kinds of economic systems are *market, command,* and *traditional.*
Student Language:	An economic system is used by a country to decide how to produce and distribute goods and services. Every country has some kind of economic system.
Example:	The economic system of the United States is primarily a market economy because the prices of goods, services, and productive resources guide most economic activity.
Attention!	No economy is purely market, command, or traditional. Economies contain elements of all three, although one will be predominate.

Profit

Content Statement: Profit is the difference between the sales revenues and all the costs of producing a good or service.

Student Language: When you produce and sell a good or service, your profit is the difference between the money you make when you sell it and all your costs of production.

Example: Willie received $200 from selling lemonade. He figured all his costs were $125. His profit was $75.

Role of Government

Content Statement: The main role of government in a market economy is to 1. provide a legal framework, 2. ensure competition, 3. provide public goods, such as roads and national defense, and 4. control "market failures," such as pollution and animal extinction.

Government is financed through taxation.

Student Language: The main roles of government in an economy are:
1. Provide laws to help the economy run smoothly
2. Make sure there is enough competition among businesses.
3. Provide public goods, such as roads and national defense.
4. Control bad effects of production, such as pollution, and preserve endangered resources through such things as wildlife protection.

Government gets money by collecting *taxes*.

Example: Enforcing business contracts through the legal system is an important role that government plays in the United States economy.

International Trade

Content Statement:

International trade is the exchange of goods and services among people and institutions in different nations. Voluntary trade increases specialization and competition and gives people a broader range of choices of goods and services. Consumers in nations who engage in international trade increase their overall standard of living.

Exports are domestic goods and services that are sold to buyers in other nations.

Imports are goods and services that are bought from sellers in other nations.

Quotas and *tariffs* are common barriers to trade.

Student Language:

International trade is the exchange of goods and services between countries. Trade among countries, like trade among people, increases specialization, competition, and world production.

Exports are goods and services produced in one country and then sold to buyers in another.

Imports are goods and services bought from sellers in other countries.

Nations sometimes use *quotas* (limits on imports) and *tariffs* (taxes on imports) to limit international trade.

Example:

The United States imports coffee and exports wheat.

Attention!

The issue of international trade is often controversial. It is true that some workers in specific industries may be hurt by trade. For example, some American clothing workers have had to change jobs during the past 25 years because of clothing imports. However, this trade allows Americans to buy quality clothing at good prices, resulting in a higher standard of living for the U.S. and for our trading partners. For this reason, most economists agree that it is good to let countries trade as much as possible. Indeed, international trade is growing throughout the world.

Circular Flow Model

Content Statement:
The circular flow model of a pure market economy illustrates the interactions of households and businesses in three markets: products (good and services), productive resources, and financial capital.

Student Language:
The circular flow model shows how households, businesses, and financial institutions (such as banks) interact as they exchange goods and services.

Example:

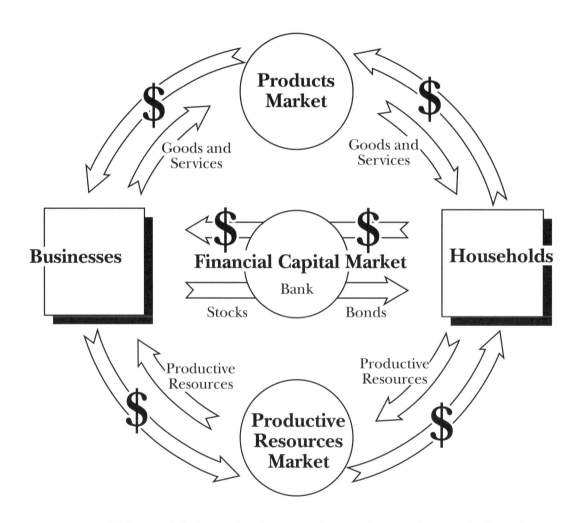

Attention!

This model shows businesses borrowing savings only from households. In reality, the situation is more complex since businesses as well as households provide savings to the market. Also, consumers and governments compete with businesses to borrow the available savings.

With younger children, you do not need to show the financial capital market.

Part 2

Teaching Activities

Based on Popular Children's Stories

Charlie Needs a Cloak
By Tomie de Paola

Summary

Charlie and his favorite sheep produce a good — a new cloak. Students learn about the different productive resources (natural, human, and capital) that Charlie uses. Charlie does not specialize in his production — he does all the production steps himself (unit production).

Key Economic Concepts

Productive Resources   Natural Resources
Human Resources   Capital Resources
Specialization

Materials

Handouts 1 and 2

 ## Teaching Procedure

1. Carefully describe and explain the different productive resources using the *Production Model*. (See Part 1 — Economic Concepts.) For younger students, this may take several short lessons. Try to show examples of real tools, cut out pictures of resources from magazines, etc.

2. As you read the story, tell students to mentally note examples of productive resources.

3. Divide the class into groups of three. On Handout 1, classify the productive resources found in the story. (Younger students may want to draw pictures.)

   Another option is to have students make index cards of the specific productive resources found in the story and then put them on the board under the correct productive resource category.

4. Gather all students together and in turn have each group share an example of a productive resource that they listed on Handout 1. Continue until all resources have been identified. Record group responses on the board.

5. Have students complete Handout 2, "Pumpkin Producers."

Key Questions To Ask Students

1. Was Charlie producing a **good** or **service**? *(good)*

2. What are some examples of other kinds of goods and services? *(Answers will vary.)*

3. What are some of the **productive resources** Charlie used to make his cloak? *(natural — land, wood for energy, any natural resources that went into making raw materials or capital resources; human — Charlie's labor; capital — pot, scissors, needle, etc.)*

4. Did Charlie specialize in making his cloak? *(No, he did everything himself. He did <u>not</u> **divide the labor**. He engaged in **unit production**.)*

 Follow-Up Activities

1. *Play Dough Production:* Give each student a small piece of play dough. Have students do some or all of these tasks:

   - Make an example of a natural resource.
   - Make an example of a capital resource.
   - Show someone (a human resource!) producing a good or service.

2. *Pat Your Head, Clap Your Hands, and Stomp Your Feet!* In a large group, call out the names of various productive resources. If you call out a natural resource, students must pat their heads. If you call out a human resource, they must clap their hands; a capital resource, and they must stomp their feet.

3. *Design a Factory:* Have students draw peanut-butter-and-jelly sandwiches being made inside their own specially-designed "Peanut-Butter-and-Jelly Sandwich Factory." Show people working at various jobs and also show various types of capital resources being used. Be creative and have fun!

Productive Resources

Charlie (and his pet sheep!) needed productive resources to produce his cloak. Discuss the story with your group. List as many productive resources as you can that Charlie used. List them under the correct type of productive resource — either natural, human, or capital.

Natural Resources (Raw Materials)	Human Resources	Capital Resources

In real life, how do people get productive resources? _____

_____

_____

_____

Pumpkin Producers

In the columns below, identify the resources necessary to produce pumpkins.

Natural Resources (Raw Materials)	Human Resources	Capital Resources

Write a paragraph describing how to produce pumpkins. Be sure to discuss productive resources! Give your paragraph a title and use your best writing. Use correct spelling and punctuation.

TITLE: _____

_____

_____

_____

_____

_____

The Giving Tree
By Shel Silverstein

Summary

This is a tender story about a tree and a boy. The tree loves the boy so much that it is willing to give the boy everything that it has (apples, shade, branches, and trunk). This story represents the ultimate sacrifice of love and the serene acceptance of another's capacity to love in return.

Key Economic Concepts   Natural Resources   Economic Wants
                             Scarcity   Price

Materials   Handouts 1, 2, and 3

 Teaching Procedure

1. Carefully read and discuss this story with your students. Define and discuss the words sacrifice, natural resource, and scarcity.

2. Using Handout 1, have students make a list of all the natural resources that the tree gave to the boy and how the boy used them for his own benefit. Point out how the boy's wants changed as he grew older. Have students identify their various wants and list them on the board.

3. Explain the concept of **scarcity**. Divide the class into three groups and have the students make a list of natural resources. Compare the lists and discuss the concept of scarcity as it applies to natural resources. *(Natural resources are scarce because most are not <u>freely</u> available to anyone who wants them. An exception is sunshine.)*

4. Discuss how some things are **more scarce** than others. Explain that the **price** of something reveals how scarce it is compared to other things.

5. In large print, write the word APPRECIATE across the blackboard. Discuss the importance of being appreciative. Ask the students if they feel the boy showed appreciation towards the tree. How does appreciation of our natural resources help us to make better choices?

6. On Handout 2, have students write a note of appreciation to the tree. Then have students write a note of appreciation to someone who has sacrificed something for them (mother, father, teacher, grandparent, person in the armed services, etc.).

7. List **goods** (products) that are directly related to apple trees (wood, apple pies, caramel apples, applesauce, cider, apple juice, apple butter, etc.). Discuss why these goods are all **scarce**.

8. Complete Handout 3, the Writers Journal for The Giving Tree.

 Key Questions To Ask Students

1. What are **natural resources**? *(gifts of nature, source of raw materials)*
   Why are natural resources **scarce**? *(not enough for everyone to have all they want)*

2. In the marketplace, how can you tell if one resource (or **good**) is **more scarce** than another? *(Its **price** gives the clue!)* Give examples.

3. Discuss the differences between **renewable** and **non-renewable** resources.

4. What are the **economic wants** in this story? Did the boy really need all the tree gave him? What are the consequences when we lose control of our wants? *(We purchase goods and services we cannot afford. We may get into too much debt.)*

5. Did the boy appreciate the tree's sacrifices? How does appreciation help us make better choices?

 Follow-Up Activities

1. *Play Dough Production:* Make examples of natural resources using play dough.

2. *Bulletin Board:* Create a bulletin board using the headings "Renewable Resources" and "Non-Renewable Resources." Cut out and categorize pictures from magazines.

3. *Johnny Appleseed:* Study Johnny Appleseed and other apple facts.

4. *Field Trip:* Visit an apple orchard. Discuss the natural, capital, and human resources used to produce apples.

5. *Kids in the Kitchen:* Make an apple pie. Read and discuss the story, *How To Make an Apple Pie*, by Marjorie Priceman.

The Giving Tree Chart

Stages of Boy's Life	Tree's Gift to the Boy	How the Boy Used Each Resource
Little Boy		
Young Man		
Man		
Older Man		
Old Man		

Thank You Letters

Dear Giving Tree,

_____

_____

_____

_____

_____

_____

Thank you,

_____

* *

Dear _____

_____

_____

_____

_____

_____

_____

Thank you,

_____

Writer's Journal for *The Giving Tree*

1. In your own words, tell what the economic word **scarcity** means.

_____

_____

_____

2. Write a sentence describing the **scarcity** situation in *The Giving Tree*.

_____

_____

3. In your own words, tell how the tree felt about giving up most of its natural resources, goods, and services. Did giving make the tree happy? Was the tree happy at the end of the story?

_____

_____

_____

_____

4. Did the boy understand and appreciate the tree's sacrifice for him? Explain.

_____

_____

_____

_____

The Doorbell Rang
By Pat Hutchins

Summary

The Doorbell Rang is a story that emphasizes the spirit of giving. It is an amusing story of two children about to eat a dozen cookies. Each time the children are about to eat their cookies, the doorbell rings. Each ring of the doorbell brings more and more children. The cookies have to be redistributed each time. This lesson is an excellent way to introduce the concept of scarcity.

Key Economic Concepts   Scarcity   Productive Resources

Materials   Handouts 1 and 2

 Teaching Procedure

1. Carefully read and discuss this story with your students. Discuss and give examples of the economic concept of **scarcity**.

2. Discuss how the concept of scarcity applies to the story. What would have happened if grandmother hadn't brought the children another batch of cookies? *(Cookies would be even more scarce!)*

3. On Handout 1, have students color the dozen cookies on the sheet, cut them out, and use them to act out the story. Reinforce the concept of scarcity as they divide up the cookies each time the doorbell rings.

4. Using Handout 2, have students complete the Writer's Journal.

 Key Questions To Ask Students

1. What is **scarcity**? *(It means not having enough of something for everyone to have all they want — at a zero price.)* Why is scarcity a problem for the children in the story? *(There are not enough cookies!)*

2. Suppose each child in the story has a cookie. Could cookies still be **scarce**? *(Yes! There, still may not enough for children to have all they want! In fact, even if all wants for cookies are satisfied in a particular situation, economists still classify cookies as a scarce good! This is because they must be produced from scarce resources which have alternative uses. They are not freely available to everyone who wants them.)*

3. When scarce **goods** are sold in stores, what do they always have? (a **price**) How do we know if one good is more scarce than another? (*higher price*)

4. Can you think of anything that is *not* **scarce**? (*saltwater at the beach, garbage, sand in the desert*) Why? (*They are freely available. There is enough for everyone to have all they want!*)

5. What **natural resources (raw materials), human resources**, and **capital resources** are used in this story to make cookies?

 Follow-Up Activities

1. *Play Dough Production*: Give each child some play dough. Have each student produce a dozen play dough cookies. Read the story out loud and have students divide up the play dough cookies to accompany the story.

2. *Kids in the Kitchen Economics*: Have students make a batch of chocolate chip cookies. As the class is baking cookies, identify the natural resources (raw materials), human resources, and capital resources used to make cookies.

3. *Scarcity List*: Brainstorm and identify things that can be listed under the headings of "Scarce Goods" and "Scarce Services."

4. *Field Trip*: Visit a bakery and analyze the production process. In the classroom, draw, label, and write a paragraph describing how baked goods are produced from productive resources.

The Doorbell Rang!

Create a dozen of your favorite kind of cookies. Color, decorate, and cut them out. Use the cookies to show how they were divided up in the story, *The Doorbell Rang*. On a separate sheet of paper, write about all of the **productive resources** that would go into making a real batch of cookies.

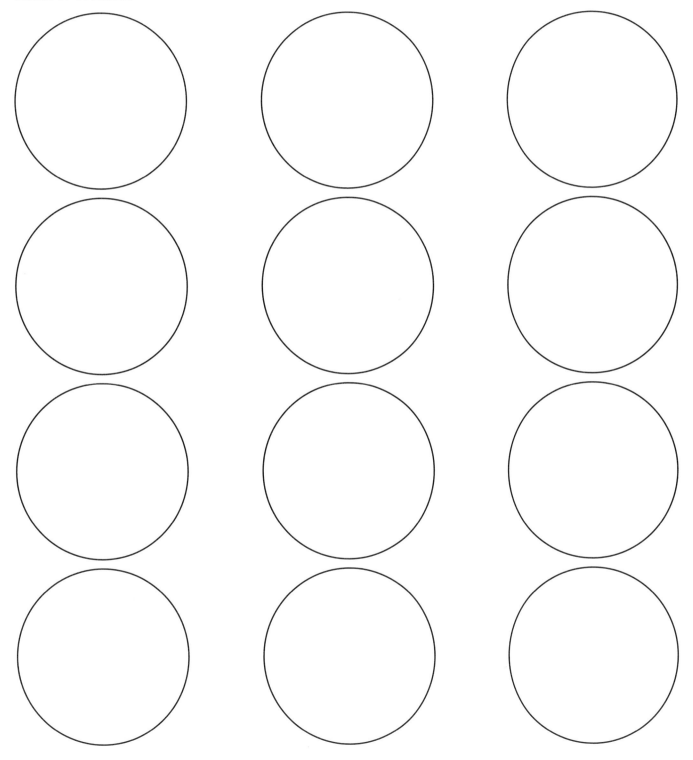

Writer's Journal — *The Doorbell Rang*!

1. Tell how you think Sam and Victoria felt when they experienced the problem of scarcity? Did they like dividing up the cookies?

   _____

   _____

   _____

   _____

2. How can you tell if a good is very scarce or not very scarce? On a separate piece of paper, draw a picture to go with your explanation.

   _____

   _____

   _____

   _____

3. Cut out pictures and paste them under these two headings:

   Very Scarce Goods   <u>Not</u> **Very Scarce Goods**

Arthur's Pet Business
By Marc Brown

Summary

To prove he is responsible enough to own a pet and to repay a debt of money to his sister, Arthur decides to start a pet business — providing pet care service to community members. He advertises by putting up signs around the neighborhood. Business is very good. Arthur not only earns a profit (from which he pays his debt) but also gains a pet when one of his "clients" has puppies under his bed.

Key Economic Concepts

Goods
Income
Choices
Profit

Services
Wages
Entrepreneur

Materials

Handouts 1 and 2

Teaching Procedure

1. Describe the differences and similarities between **goods** and **services**. Reproduce two copies of Handout 1. Title one hotel GOODS and the other SERVICES. Have students cut pictures from magazines or draw pictures of goods and services and glue them to the correct hotel.

2. As students read the story, have them identify goods and services shown in the illustrations or mentioned in the story. (These could be added or drawn on the Hotel Handouts above.)

3. Define **entrepreneur**. Discuss how Arthur fits this definition.

4. Give each student five copies of Handout 2 — Income Interview. Students should interview at least five people at home or in the community. They should ask what work the people do to earn an **income** and then complete the interview form.

5. As a class, analyze and discuss the data collected in the interviews. Determine which people provide a **good** and which provide a **service**. Were any of the people interviewed entrepreneurs? Discuss why or why not.

Key Questions To Ask Students

1. What were Arthur's job choices? *(work in a bank or a junk yard)*

2. Why did Arthur start a business? *(to earn **income** so he could repay a debt and prove he was responsible enough to own a pet)*

3. What is the difference between a **good** and a **service**? *(A good is a tangible item; a service is something someone does for another person.)*

4. Was Arthur providing a good or a service? *(service)*

5. Is Arthur considered an entrepreneur? *(yes)* Why? *(He made the choice to organize and manage a business.)*

6. Do you think it is more difficult being an **entrepreneur** or working for someone else? Why? Why do people want to be entrepreneurs? *(Probably more difficult being an entrepreneur. Must organize all the productive resources. Must be willing to take a **risk**. Always requires long hours and much dedication. People like being their own boss. Possibility for much **profit**.)*

 ## Follow-Up Activities

1. *Field Trip:* Go to the businesses of people interviewed and have students take photos of them at work. Attach photos to Handout 1 and make a class booklet called "Community Providers of Goods and Services."

2. *Charades:* On slips of paper, put examples of goods and services. Have a student draw a slip and act out how to produce the good or service. The class guesses what job it is and whether it provides a good or a service.

3. *Start a Classroom Business:* Try one that provides a good and then one that provides a service. Compare and contrast. For example: a. Make packets of note cards with matching envelopes. b. Be "envelope stuffers" for the principal, school secretary, lunch supervisor, or other teachers.

4. *It's All in the Advertising!* Have students choose an occupation or business that interests them and make posters advertising it.

Income Interview

REPORTER _____

PERSON INTERVIEWED _____

1. What **good** or **service** do you produce to earn an income?

2. Do you work by yourself or do you work as part of a group? If you work as part of a group, what are the good and bad points about working this way?

3. What **capital resources** (tools, machinery, equipment, etc.) do you use?

4. What special training or skills (**human capital**) do you need to do your job well?

5. How did you decide to do this kind of work? Would you recommend this kind of work to others? Why or why not?

PANCAKES, PANCAKES!
By Eric Carle

Summary

This is a story about a boy named Jack who wakes up with an enormous appetite for pancakes. His mother informs him that before she can make pancakes, he must first gather all the necessary ingredients. Jack must cut the wheat, take it to the miller, have the wheat ground, and gather the eggs — a step-by-step process for making pancakes the old-fashioned way!

Key Economic Concepts	Specialization	Division of Labor
	Interdependence	Productive Resources
	Market	

Materials	Handouts 1 and 2

 ## Teaching Procedure

1. Carefully read and discuss the story with your students. Explain these concepts: specialization, division of labor, and interdependence. Reinforce the idea that raw materials come from natural resources. Discuss natural, human, and capital resources as related to this story.

2. Using Handout 1, have students classify vocabulary words from *Pancakes, Pancakes!* — under appropriate concept column.

3. Complete Handout 2, the Writer's Journal for *Pancakes, Pancakes!*

4. Working in small groups, list all the people it took to make the pancakes. *(specialization)* Discuss the concepts of specialization and interdependence. Emphasize that when people specialize they always become more dependent on one another. *(interdependence)*

Key Questions To Ask Students

1. What is the difference between **natural**, **human**, and **capital resources**?

2. Define **specialization** and **interdependence**. How does the term **division of labor** apply in this story? How does specialization affect economic production? *(It increases **productivity** and, therefore, the quantity of goods and services produced. It standardizes production.)* Does specialization make someone more or less dependent on others? *(more)*

3. What are some ways people **specialize** in your community? How does this make people in your community **interdependent**? *(People must depend on one another to provide goods and services.)*

4. What is a **market**? Brainstorm examples of different markets. *(stores, city markets, auctions, stock markets, etc.)* How are they different? How are they the same? *(They always help buyers and sellers get together to exchange and to determine prices.)*

5. How do rural **markets** in less developed countries differ from marketplaces such as large department stores in the United States? *(haggling for prices, goods often displayed on ground, sometimes takes place only one or two days each week, etc.)*

6. When your family makes pancakes, do you follow all the steps in the story? Why not? *(It would take too much **scarce** time!)* How do **markets** help you make pancakes? *(You can easily buy ingredients that others produce. You can even buy complete pancake mixes!)*

 ## Follow-Up Activities

1. *Flow Chart*: Design a pancake production flow chart to go with this story.

2. *Kids in the Kitchen*: Make pancakes with your students and enjoy breakfast together. Have students list different items they could put into or on their pancakes to change the taste.

3. *Maple Syrup*: Do a teaching unit on maple syrup. Research information on how maple syrup is produced. Make a flow chart illustrating this process.

4. *How Other Products Are Produced*: Research how other products are produced. Research ingredients and the production process. Create your own story! (i.e., "Hot Dogs, Hot Dogs"; "Popcorn, Popcorn"; or "Soda, Soda.")

PANCAKES, PANCAKES!

1. Put the following vocabulary words in the correct column:

   wheat, donkey, miller, stone, water, Jack, water wheel, egg, hen, milk, plate, cow, pail, fire, firewood, mixing bowl, wooden spoon, frying pan, mother, flail

   Watch out! Some of them may be tricky! (For example, is a donkey a natural resource or a capital resource?)

NATURAL RESOURCES (Raw Materials)	HUMAN RESOURCES (Labor)	CAPITAL RESOURCES

2. On the back of this paper, draw pictures of natural, human, and capital resources.

Writer's Journal — *PANCAKES, PANCAKES!*

1. In your own words, explain what **specialization** means. *Why* do people specialize?

   _____

   _____

   _____

2. From the story, list at least three examples of **specialization**.

   _____

   _____

   _____

3. List all the steps Jack took in gathering the **ingredients** necessary for making pancakes.

   _____

   _____

   _____

   _____

   _____

   _____

4. On the back of this paper, draw and color a delicious plate of pancakes.

The Goat in the Rug
By Charles L. Blood and Martin Link

Summary

Geraldine the goat literally puts her whole self into the weaving of a Navajo rug. After being sheared for her wool, she watches as Glenmae cleans, dries, combs, spins, and dyes her wool. Geraldine is so proud! A lot of her is in that rug. She hopes to grow her wool quickly so she can be a part of the next Navajo rug.

Key Economic Concepts

Unit Production   Specialization
Assembly Line   Division of Labor
Interdependence   Productivity

Materials

Handouts 1 and 2   Ruler
Glue   Scissors
Construction Paper (various colors)

Teaching Procedure

1. After reading the story, define and discuss **unit production** (when one person produces the complete product). Point out that Glenmae did all the steps herself in the rug's production. Discuss how long this process could have taken. Use the illustrations of the story showing the regrowth of Geraldine's wool as an indicator of the passage of time.

2. Explain **division of labor**, **specialization**, **interdependence**, and **assembly line**.

3. (Optional) Illustrate these concepts by making "hamburgers" using Lesson 8 from the *Play Dough Economics* curriculum. (www.ncee.net)

4. Using Handout 1, have students create a paper "rug." Follow these steps:
   a. Prepare a 9" x 12" sheet of construction paper to use as a "loom."
   b. Measure and cut ten 1" x 9" strips of paper in various colors.
   c. Students weave paper strips on the loom and glue down all ends.

   Note starting and completion time.

5. For the assembly line part of Handout 1, assign jobs to several students:
   ___ paper folders for looms   ___ paper measurers for strips
   ___ paper measures for looms   ___ paper cutters for strips
   ___ paper cutters for looms   ___ 10 paper weavers
   ___ paper ends gluers   ___ quality control person

6. Specify some total number of minutes for **unit** and **assembly line production**. Compare and contrast the production results.

7. Using Handout 2, have students design their own assembly lines to make a product (e.g. ice cream sandwiches, cookies, Christmas ornaments).

 Key Questions To Ask Students

1. Was Glenmae producing a **good** or a **service**? *(a good)*

2. Did Glenmae **specialize** in making the rug? *(No, she did everything herself. She engaged in unit production.)*

3. How long was the **production** time in the making of the rug? *(several weeks)* Why? *(Glenmae did all the work herself.)*

4. When people **specialize**, as on an assembly line, they become more **interdependent**. What does this mean? *(They depend more on one another.)*

5. What is the main advantage of **specializing** in producing goods and services? *(increased productivity — i.e. more output per unit of input.)* What are some disadvantages? *(Work can be repetitive and tedious. If one person is sick or leaves, others may not be able to do the work.)*

 Follow-Up Activities

1. *Field Trip Time!* Take a field trip to a candy factory or a bakery that uses assembly line production. Also try to visit a small business that produces the same products using unit production. Compare and contrast.

2. *How Much Does It Cost?* Compare the cost of mass-produced products to those made using unit production. Are they the same? Are they different? What would account for this?

3. *Can It Be Done?* Can *services* be produced using an assembly line? Can they be produced using a *specialized* process that divides the labor? Visit a local electric company or water company and discuss these concepts during your visit. Or, have a company representative visit your classroom.

Making a Paper Navajo Rug

NAME _____

UNIT PRODUCTION

Steps necessary to produce a "rug:"

1. Create Paper "loom" (9" x 12")
2. Cut 10 Strips (1" x 9")
3. Weave Strips
4. Glue Ends

Amount of Time Used for Production: _____

Number of Rugs Produced Per Unit of Time: _____
(i.e. Productivity)

ASSEMBLY LINE PRODUCTION

Number of People on the Assembly Line: _____

Amount of Time Used for Production: _____

Number of Rugs Produced: _____

Number of Rugs Produced Per Person _____

Rugs Produced Per Unit of Time (Per Person) _____
(i.e. Productivity)

Design Your Own Assembly Line

NAME _____

Design your own **assembly line** for making English muffin pizzas or fruit salad.

Brainstorm ideas of **goods** to produce. Choose one and design an **assembly line** for its production.

Mitchell Is Moving
By Marjorie Weinman Sharmat

Summary

Mitchell the dinosaur is bored and wants to move away. His decision to move costs him something, something very important left behind. Mitchell solves the dilemma, builds a new home, and keeps an old friend.

Key Economic Concepts

Choices
Scarcity
Human Resources
Capital Resources

Opportunity Cost
Productive Resources
Natural Resources

Materials

Handouts 1 and 2

Scissors and Yarn

 ## Teaching Procedure

1. Following the reading of the story, discuss Mitchell's two choices: to move or to stay.

2. Explain **opportunity cost**, giving examples. Discuss the decision Mitchell made and his opportunity cost.

3. Using Handout 1, tell students to pretend they are moving away in two weeks with Mitchell. They may take only one suitcase. Have students list, draw, or cut out magazine pictures of what they would like to take in the suitcase.

4. Explain that due to a **scarcity** (be sure to define this) of space, they may only choose two items to take with them. Have the students circle the two items on their suitcase.

5. In small groups, have the students explain their choices.

6. Since all students will be living with Mitchell in one hut, tell them that they can now only take one item, again due to a **scarcity** of space. Have students choose the one item and explain their choice. Identify the **opportunity cost** of each choice.

7. Using Handout 2, have students write their choice and their opportunity cost on the appropriate tag.

8. Have students color and cut out the suitcases and luggage tags. Attach tags to suitcases with yarn. Display on a bulletin board.

Key Questions To Ask Students

1. What **choices** did Mitchell have? *(to move or to stay, what to pack in his suitcase)*

2. Why did he have to make a choice? *(**Scarcity**! He couldn't both move away and stay.)*

3. What did he decide? *(He decided to move.)* What was his **opportunity cost?** *(He had to give up all the benefits of staying — including being next to Margo!)*

4. If Mitchell had decided to stay instead of move, what would have been his opportunity **cost**? *(He would have given up all the benefits of moving away — new bedroom, house, and kitchen, nice and slimy moss, nice and mucky swamp water, etc.)*

5. Mitchell had to pack his suitcase. Could he have chosen to keep putting in even more things that he wanted to bring? *(No. Eventually he would run out of space and he would have to make a choice about what to take.)*

6. What **productive resources** did Mitchell use when making his new hut? *(natural — stones, large boulders, trees, bushes, mud, flowers, wood; human — himself; capital — tools to put doorknob on and to plant flowers)*

7. Identify which of these **productive resources** are **human**, **capital**, or **natural**?

 Follow-Up Activities

1. *Build a House!* Divide the class into small groups and give each group a baggie of assorted items such as: small amount of clay, yarn, paper clips, rubber bands, squares of paper, Popsicle sticks, toothpicks, small pebbles, or beads. As a group, students should build a house with the items in the baggie. Following the activity, discuss scarcity and productive resources.

2. *My Scarcity Situations*: Complete the "My Scarcity Situations" worksheet in Part 3, page 143.

3. *Bulletin Board:* Have your students create an "Opportunity Cost" bulletin board.

4. *Econ and Me*: View and discuss the "Opportunity Cost" lesson from the *Econ and Me* video series. (www.ncee.net)

Mitchell Is Moving

Name _____

Mitchell Is Moving

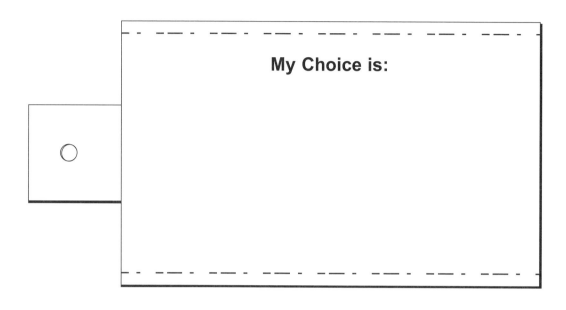

My Choice is:

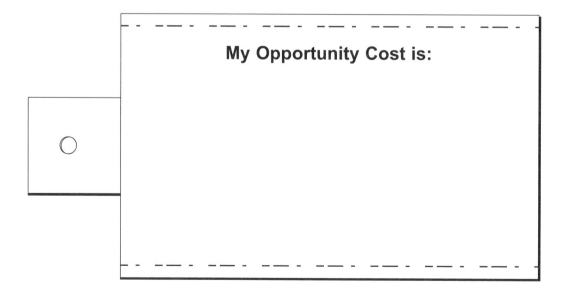

My Opportunity Cost is:

Uncle Jed's Barbershop
By Margaret King Mitchell

Summary

Uncle Jed's Barbershop is a heartwarming story about a barber who travels the countryside cutting poor folks' hair. Uncle Jed has a kind heart and a giving spirit. He lives for the day that he can own his own barbershop. It takes a long time and many setbacks before his lifelong dream is fulfilled. This is a wonderful story that emphasizes the true spirit of sacrifice, love, and commitment to a dream.

Key Economic Concepts

Specialization   Opportunity Cost
Savings   Investing

Materials

Handouts 1, 2, and 3

Teaching Procedure

1. Carefully read and discuss this story with your students. Define the words sacrifice, specialization, and opportunity cost.

2. Discuss the economic concepts of **specialization** and **opportunity cost** and how they relate to Uncle Jed.

3. On Handout 1, complete the chart by identifying special services provided by the businesses. After students finish, discuss why businesses **specialize** in the goods and services they produce.

4. Have students complete the Writer's Journal, Handout 2.

5. Complete Handout 3, *My Opportunity Costs*. Divide students into small groups to discuss their opportunity costs.

Key Questions to Ask Students

1. Did Uncle Jed produce a **good** or a **service**? (*service*)

2. How did Uncle Jed get money to help with Sarah Jean's operation and start his barber shop? *(He had to **save**. This means not consuming in the present in order to consume later on.)*

3. What is **opportunity cost**? (*The best alternative you give up when you make a choice.*) What was Uncle Jed's opportunity cost when he decided to use his savings to help Sarah Jean? (*giving up using his savings to purchase his barber shop*) What was the opportunity cost of a decision you made?

4. What does it mean to **specialize**? (*working in jobs where you produce a few special goods or services*) How are the terms **specialization** and careers related? (*People specialize when they choose their particular line of work.*) Discuss why a community needs people doing many specialized jobs. What would our community be like if no one wanted to specialize in medicine, education, business, etc.?

5. At the end of the story, Uncle Jed invested his savings and started his barber shop. What does it mean to **invest**? (*People invest when they use their savings to purchase capital equipment to start or expand a business. People also invest when they acquire skills and knowledge through education and training.*)

6. What **capital resources** did he acquire to start his barbershop? (*building, barber chairs, mirrors, barber tools, etc.*)

7. Are we ever too old to fulfill our dreams? Uncle Jed was 79 years old when his dream came true. Can you think of others who had to wait until old age to fulfill their dreams? (*Grandma Moses, Col. Sanders of Kentucky Fried Chicken*) What are your dreams? What special **good** or **service** do you want to produce when you grow up? What education or special training **(human capital)** will you need to fulfill your dream?

 Follow-Up Activities

1. *Play Dough Economics:* Give each child a piece of play dough. Have them show someone specializing as he or she produces a **service**.

2. *Career Day:* Have a career day where members of the community speak about their careers. Have students research and write about what good or service they want to provide when they grow up. Discuss what effect their career could have on their community. (This is a good time to discuss economic *interdependence*.) Also have students identify special skills, education, and training **(human capital)** needed for certain jobs.

3. *Recording Opportunity Costs:* Have students record in their journals the opportunity cost of the decisions they made during a day. This helps students become aware of how many daily decisions they make and what they must give up with each decision. Students can use the "My Scarcity Situations" handout from Part 3, page 143.

Special Services in Our Community

BUSINESS	SPECIAL SERVICE
Beauty Salon	
Doctor's Office	
Auto Repair Shop	
Realtor's Office	
Photo Store	
Lawn Care Business	
Hospital	
Tailor Shop	
Florist Shop	
Dry Cleaners	
Lawyer's Office	
Plumber's Shop	

Writer's Journal for Uncle Jed's Barbershop

1. In your own words, tell how you think Uncle Jed felt about giving up all his **savings** for Sarah Jane's operation.

   _____

   _____

   _____

   _____

   _____

2. Write four words that describe Uncle Jed's personality.

   _____   _____

   _____   _____

3. What **good** or **service** would you like to produce when you grow up? Write about your special dream.

   _____

   _____

   _____

   _____

4. What education or special training (**human capital**) will it take to fulfill your dream?

   _____

   _____

   _____

   _____

My Opportunity Costs

A Decision I Made	**My Opportunity Cost**
1. _____	_____
2. _____	_____
3. _____	_____
4. _____	_____
5. _____	_____
6. _____	_____
7. _____	_____

Which decision was the most difficult for you? _____

_____

Why was it the most difficult? _____

_____

_____

Draw a picture showing you making a difficult decision. Write a paragraph describing this decision. In the paragraph, identify your opportunity cost.

Ant Cities
By Arthur Dorros

Summary

This is a nonfiction story about different kinds of ants and how they live and work together. Ants live in colonies, and all ants have particular jobs to do, much like workers in our cities. Working together, ants keep their "cities" growing and surviving almost anywhere.

Key Economic Concepts

Jobs   Income
Workers   Services
Taxes   Government
Producers

Materials

Handouts 1 and 2   Candy Treats
Materials for the folder activity

 ## Teaching Procedure

1. While reading the story, compare the types of ants and their **specific jobs** to workers in your own community.

2. After reading the story, complete Handout 1.

3. Explain that certain **services** (jobs) are often performed by government agencies. Give examples: police officers, trash collectors, judges, highway workers, etc.

4. Review why people have jobs: to earn money (income) to purchase **goods** and **services.**

5. Discuss **taxes.** Explain that citizens pay taxes to the government which in turn provides certain goods and services. Government also pays government workers salaries and wages with the taxes.

6. Refer to Handout 1 and identify the community jobs that are often provided by government agencies. Discuss which of these jobs can also be provided by private businesses. (water, trash, etc.)

7. Using Handout 2, let each student color, cut out, and count their money. Tell students this is their weekly pay. They can use it to buy some candy treats. But wait! First they must pay for certain **government services**. Collect $ .50 for road repair, $1.00 for police and fire protection, and $ .75 for trash pick-up. As each transaction takes place, students should calculate how much pay is left. Let students buy candy treats with their remaining money. Discuss the activity.

8. Have students do the Public or Private? (or Both!) activity, Handout 3.

Key Questions To Ask Students

1. What are the **jobs** of some of the ants? *(harvester, workers, etc.)*

2. Do they provide **goods** or **services**? *(services)*

3. How do these jobs compare to jobs in your community? *(highway workers, trash collectors, grain elevator workers, builders, pest controllers, cooks, moms, armed services, police, etc.)*

4. How are your community workers paid? *(They earn income by earning wages.)*

5. When people work at their jobs, are they **producers** or **consumers**? *(producers)*

6. Where does the money come from to pay these **wages**? *(private employers, taxes, collected by government)*

7. Why do people pay **taxes**? *(to pay for certain services that may not be provided sufficiently by private businesses: police protection, national defense, roads)*

8. Discuss different types of taxes. *(income, sales, property, excise, etc.)*

 ## Follow-Up Activities

1. Design Your Own Money. Use a blank form and have students design their own currency for use in a class mini-economy.

2. Visit a local government office or department. Take a field trip to the local trash, water, highway, fire, or police departments. Visit the mayor, city hall, or a local legislator. Create a class book on the jobs students learned about.

3. Find out the amount of city or county taxes raised in your area. What kind of taxes are they? Once taxes are paid, where does the money go? Who receives the tax payments?

4. Write a letter to a city or county worker (public employee) asking about his or her job. With classmates, compile a book on public employees.

5. Write a letter to the mayor, city or county council, or newspaper editor stating your position on city or county taxes. Should they be raised or lowered? Why or why not?

Ants and Community Workers
How Do They Compare?

Name _____

Complete the table below referring to the story if needed. List the types of ants, what job each ant performs, and who in your own community might perform that kind of job.

Type of Ant	Job It Performs	Community Worker

How Our Taxes Work!

Name _____

Hurray! Today is PAY DAY! This money is your **income** for work completed this week. You will be able to buy some candy treats with it! Color and cut out the money. Fill in the table below as directed by your teacher.

Amount You Were Paid	_____
First Tax	_____
Sub Total	_____
Second Tax	_____
Sub Total	_____
Third Tax	_____
Amount Left After All Taxes	_____

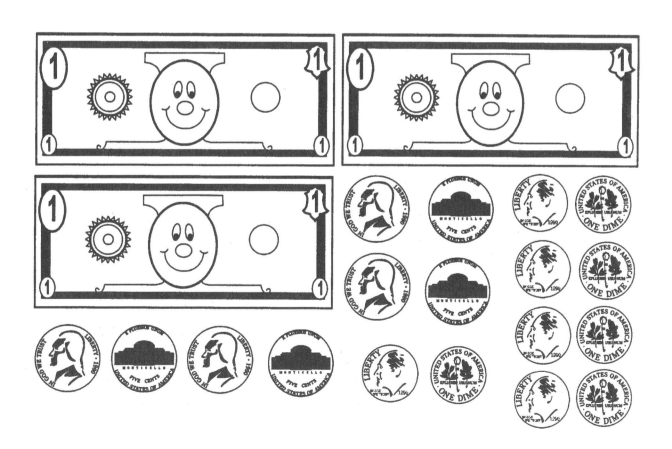

Public or Private? (or Both!)

A File Folder Activity

Most goods and services are provided by private business. However, some goods and services are provided by government through taxes. Some goods and services can be provided by *both* private businesses and government.

File Folder Activity: In this activity, students will classify services provided by private businesses or government — or both!

Create File Folder Activity:

1. On the inside of a file folder, write PUBLIC and on the other side write PRIVATE.
2. Create cards with either words and/or pictures. Place in an envelope or plastic bag.
3. Create a check sheet for answers.

Do the Activity:

1. Student takes a card from the envelope or plastic bag.
2. Student must decide if it *usually* belongs under PUBLIC or PRIVATE.
3. After all cards have been placed on file folder, student self-checks answers.
4. Student then decides which cards he or she thinks are provided by both private businesses and government (See examples below with an asterisk *.)

Examples for Cards:

PUBLIC

Police officer	Fire fighter	*Water meter reader
Coroner	*Trash collector	Road repairman
Mayor	Street cleaner	*Parks worker
City clerk	*Librarian	Sewage treatment worker
City engineer	Animal control worker	Health department nurse

PRIVATE

Beautician/barber	*Doctor	Grocer
Car dealer	Gas station owner	Bank teller
Factory worker	Druggist/Pharmacist	Pet store owner
Brick Mason	Funeral director	TV cable person
Phone repairman	*Minister	Pizzeria owner
Florist	Auto mechanic	Sports player

Follow An Ice Cream Cone Around the World
By Neale S. Godfrey

Summary

Travel around the world with the Green$treet kids as they discover what it takes to make ice cream. Through this story, students visit the places where the different ingredients in ice cream are found. There are many "billboards" in the story that provide interesting facts about ice cream.

Key Economic Concepts

Productive Resources   Interdependence
Market Price   Supply and Demand
Raw Materials

Materials

Handouts 1 & 2

Teaching Procedure

1. Discuss all of the productive resources used in ice cream production. Emphasize how we often use resources from other countries to produce ice cream. *(interdependence)*

2. Read the story once for fun. Then read it again and list on the board the ingredients found in ice cream. Discuss the "billboards" found in the story. (The billboards give interesting facts about ice cream.)

3. Using the world map, locate countries or states which have **raw materials** (which come from **natural resources)** used in the production of ice cream. Complete Handout 1 together.

4. Brainstorm and list brand names of ice cream and ice cream flavors. Discuss marketing and advertisements. What do we look for when we buy ice cream? (*good taste, nice packaging, price, etc.*) Discuss how advertising affects the **demand** for ice cream.

5. Using Handout 2, have students draw and design their own brand of ice cream. Discuss marketing concepts and techniques. Discuss the terms consumer, producer, perishable, and nonperishable.

6. Have students find the **market price** of particular brands of ice cream. Discuss differences in prices. How different are they? Why are they different?

Key Questions To Ask Students

1. Who are the **producers** in this story? Who are the **consumers**? Who **demands** ice cream? *(consumers)* Who supplies ice cream? *(producers)*

2. What are **raw materials?** *(materials and ingredients used in production)* Where do they come from? *(Raw materials ultimately come from **natural resources**. They are sometimes called intermediate goods.)*

3. Give examples of **interdependence** found in this story. Why did the ice cream producers get raw materials from other countries? *(They didn't have certain raw materials, or they could get them more cheaply from other countries. This helps keep the price of ice cream lower for consumers.)*

4. Why do **producers** sell so many different kinds of ice cream? *(They are appealing to specific tastes and preferences of consumers.)* How do producers try to get consumers to buy their ice cream? That is, how do they try to increase the **demand** for their ice cream? *(The most common way is by advertising.)*

5. What is the **market price** of a half gallon of vanilla ice cream? Why does the price vary from brand to brand and from store to store? *(Some brands are more costly to produce. Some stores, like a local convenience store, will sell at a higher price than a large, discount grocery. People will pay more for convenience because their time is **scarce**.)*

 Follow-Up Activities

1. *Grocery Shopping:* Have students go grocery shopping with their parents and list all the ice cream products, brand names, and prices they observe.

2. *Play Dough Production:* Give each student a variety of colors of play dough and have them develop a new ice cream flavor. To increase the demand for their product, students must then write a descriptive advertisement.

3. *Dairy Farm:* Visit a dairy farm or have a dairy farmer visit and talk to the students about owning a dairy farm. List all the related products that we get from cows. Read *Who Owns the Cow* by Andrew Clements.

4. *Kids in the Kitchen Day:* Make homemade ice cream. Compare the taste with ice cream bought at the store.

5. *Collage:* Make a collage (using pictures from magazines or newspaper advertisements) of a variety of ice cream products. List market prices.

Follow An Ice Cream Cone
Around the World

Raw Material	Location
Milk	_____
Sugar Cane (sugar)	_____
Orchids (vanilla beans)	_____
Cacao beans (cocoa)	_____

Draw and label **capital resources** used to produce ice cream:

What **natural resources** go into raw materials used in the production of milk?

My Ice Cream Company

Brand Name of Ice Cream: _____

Company Name: _____

Produced in: City _____   State: _____

Flavor: _____   Market Price Per Gallon: _____

Draw and design your ice cream product. Then, write a paragraph explaining why consumers should buy *your* ice cream instead of another brand! Why is your product different or better than the competition?

My Rows and Piles of Coins
By Tolulwa Mollel

Summary

A Tanzanian boy saves his coins to buy a bicycle so that he can help his parents carry goods to market. He eventually discovers that in spite of all he has saved, he still does not have nearly enough money.

Economic Concepts

Saving   Spending
Delayed benefits   Goods and Services

Materials:

My Rows and Piles of Coins game
Accounting sheets

 ## Teaching Procedure

1. Read the story and ask students the Key Questions below. Emphasize that saving forces us to forgo current consumption. It requires discipline, but allows us to save for future, more expensive purchases.

2. Create a Rows and Piles of Coins game.

   Directions for making the game using a file folder:

   a. Open file folder and make a path of circles around the inside. Place a star in one of the circles. This will be START. On the rest of the circles make R or G on each.
   b. In the center make two rectangles. One marked Green Cards and the other marked Red Cards.
   c. Create green and red construction paper cards with short scenarios. (See provided examples. Create your own cards for more or less difficult math exercises.)
   d. Make an "accounting sheet" for each player. These could be laminated so they could be used more than once.

Directions for Playing Game:

   a. Player places marker on start.
   b. Player rolls die and moves clockwise.
   c. Where marker lands, player draws appropriate card.
   d. Player calculates amount of money on accounting sheet.
   e. First person to save $25.00 is the winner. (Players do *not* go into debt. They simply go to $0 and start over.)

Key Questions To Ask Students

1. How much **money** did the boy have at the beginning of the story? *($.50 in coins)* Why do people use money? *(to help exchange goods and services)*

2. Name three **goods** that the boy saw at the market. *(Answers will vary.)*

3. Why did the boy choose to **save** his money? *(He wanted a bicycle to enjoy and to help his mother on market day.)* What was his **opportunity cost** of saving for the bicycle? *(He wasn't able to spend the money on other goods. He had to delay his desire for current consumption. This takes discipline!)*

4. What **service** did the boy provide? *(carrying goods to market for his mother)*

5. What did the boy choose to save his money for at the beginning of the story? (bicycle) At the end? *(a cart)*

6. Why do you think this goal changed? *(Since he now owned a bike, the cart was now a more important priority.)*

7. In the story, a bicycle and cart are an example of what kind of productive resource? **(capital resource)**

Follow-Up Activities

1. Visit a local bank or have a bank representative come to the classroom to discuss his or her job. Learn different facts about currency.

2. Bring in coins from different countries. Discuss how they are the same and how they are different. Research the history of coins. What are they made of? Why are most coins no longer made of silver and gold?

3. Research and discuss exchange rates with the students. Have students write a paragraph explaining why exchange rates are important in the world economy.

4. Find Tanzania on a map. Research its economy, finding out what it produces, what its natural resources are, and how far away it is from your city.

5. Write a commercial for one of the goods, foods, or animals in the story.

6. Write a personal narrative recalling a time when you saved money to buy something.

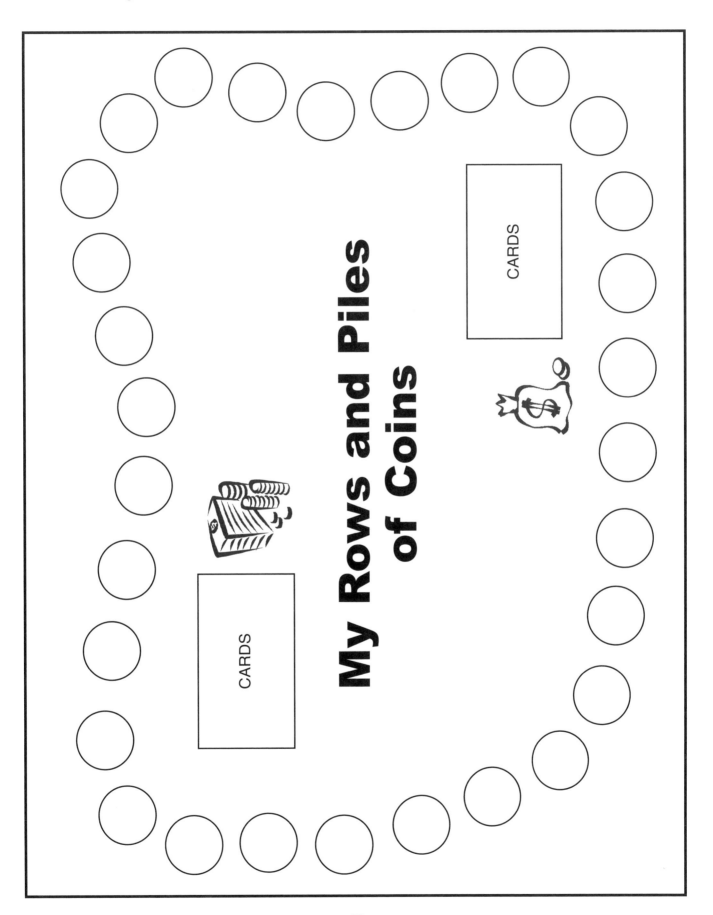

My Rows and Piles of Coins

CARDS

CARDS

My Rows and Piles of Coins "Cards"

To increase or decrease the math difficulty, create your own sets of cards.

Green Cards	Red Cards
You sold 3 CD's to a friend. You received $5.00 for them.	You had to buy lunch this week. You spend $5.00.
You earn interest on your savings account. Add $2.00.	Someone stole your wallet. You lose $5.00.
You rake leaves for a neighbor. Add $6.00.	You go to the movies with friends. Pay $6.50.
You volunteer to clean out the garage. Add $10.00.	You need a hair cut. It costs $9.50. Your mom pays half.
You shovel snow for a lady down the street. Add $5.00.	You must pay for a lost library book. Deduct $7.00.
You help to deliver newspapers for a friend. Add $3.50.	Your friend, Anna, loaned you $.50 for a lollipop last week. Pay her back.
You wash the family car. You earn $3.50.	You need 4 new pencils. The cost is $.75.
You sweep out the family car and clean all the windows inside and out. Add $2.50.	You need 3 new folders for school. You pay $1.50.
You vacuum the carpets for your mom. Earn $1.00.	Your mom says you can go to a friend's house after school, but you must take the city bus home. Pay fare of $.75.
You sell a video game you don't play any more. You get $5.50.	You stop for an after-school snack with friends at Burger Bite. Pay $2.50.

To Market, To Market
By Anne Miranda

Summary

This story, modeled after the familiar nursery rhyme about going to the market to buy a fat pig, illustrates the chaos that is created when the animals for purchase won't cooperate. Cooking a meal of homemade soup turns into quite a chore with a change in the menu!

Key Economic Concepts	Goods	Services	Raw materials
	Consumers	Producers	Market
	Productive resources (natural, human, capital)		

Materials

Handout 1 — Create a Class Book!
To Market, To Market Game board and
materials (teacher made)

 ## Teaching Procedure

1. Review basic concepts, using Key Questions To Ask Students.

2. Do the Create a Book activity, Handout 1. Each student can make an entire book or each student may contribute one page to the class book. First, explain steps for getting milk from "cow to market." Other examples for books are: tree to baseball bat, cotton to shirt, wheat to bread, etc.

3. Play the "To Market, To Market" game. This is a good evaluation tool to see if students have mastered the concepts.

 ## Key Questions To Ask Students

1. Where does this story take place? *(at the market and at the woman's home)*

2. What does the woman purchase first at the market? *(a fat pig)* When *you* go to the "market," (store) what **goods** do you purchase? *(Answers will vary.)*

3. What is a **service**? What services have you used or purchased? *(haircut, doctor, teacher, bicycle repair, police and fire protection, etc.)*

4. Is the woman a **producer** or a **consumer**? How do you know? *(She is a consumer; she purchases things at the store. Although at the end of the book she made some soup, she didn't produce it for the market.)*

5. What is a **market**? *(any place/situation where buyers and sellers interact)*

6. Why did the woman have to pay for the items she purchased at the store? *(These items/goods were **scarce**. All scarce goods have a **price**. In general, the more scarce a good or service is, the higher its price.)*

7. Why does the woman make vegetable soup? *(She was cranky and hungry after dealing with the animals!)*

8. By looking at the illustrations, name ten **goods**. *(Answers will vary.)*

9. What is the sequence of animals purchased at the market? *(pig, hen, goose, trout, lamb, cow, duck, goat)*

 Follow-Up Activities

1. Make soup using the vegetables listed in the story. Use math to double or triple the recipe so there is enough soup for the whole class.

2. Research and write a story about what it takes to grow tomatoes, make them into catsup, and then sell the catsup in stores. (Or choose another vegetable from the story.)

3. Take a field trip to a supermarket or grocery store. Prepare economics questions to ask the store owner. Write a paragraph about what you learned on the trip.

4. Make cards listing the vegetables and animals. Put cards in ABC order. Sort the cards by syllables.

5. Create your own version of "To Market, To Market" and create a nutty fruit salad. Or, create your own version of "To Market, To Market" using different animals, such as catfish, turkey, deer, squirrel, rabbit, and quail.

Handout 1
Create a Class Book!

Create a class book! Book pages will be copies of a flow chart of boxes and arrows showing how raw materials and productive resources go from "resource to market."

Example: Discuss the steps it takes for milk to go from the farm to the market. Then draw pictures and write the steps using the flow chart. (e.g. cow eats grass, milk cow, pasteurize milk, put milk on truck, deliver milk to store).

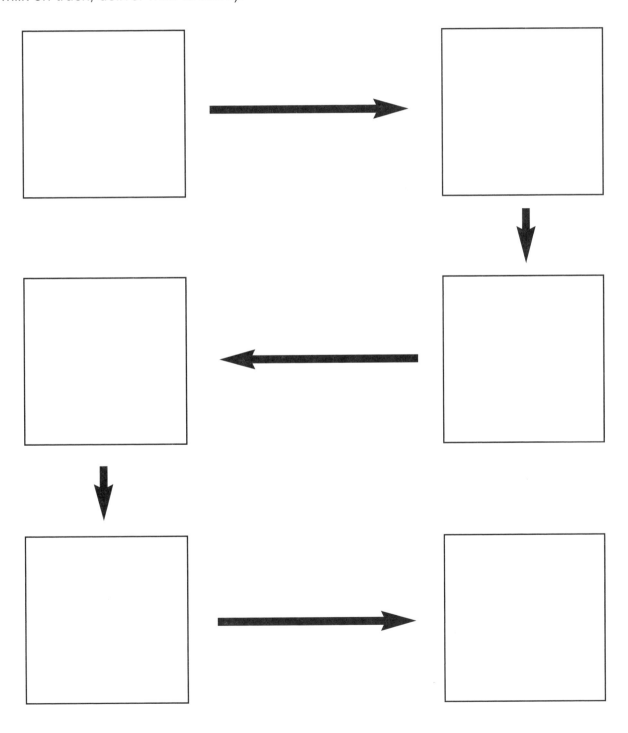

To Market To Market
Game

How To Play:

1. Place markers on start.

2. Draw a card. If the player can answer the question, then he or she rolls a die and moves the appropriate number of spaces. If the player cannot answer the question, he or she loses a turn.

3. First player to reach the market wins!

Game Preparations

- Cut out game title and paste on blank game board. Cut out directions to play game and paste in one corner of board.
- Cut out cow and paste on left of game board near the start.
- Cut out the grocery clerk and paste on the right of the game near the end of the game.
- Draw a series of shapes to create a path from the cow to the clerk.
- Write the following questions on cards:

What are goods?	Name 3 goods.
What are services?	Name 3 services or 3 people who provide services.
What is a consumer?	Name 3 consumers.
What is a producer?	Name a producer.
What are natural resources?	Name 3 natural resources.
What are human resources?	Name 3 human resources.
What are capital resources?	Name 3 capital resources.

To Market To Market

The Tortilla Factory
By Gary Paulsen

Summary

The Tortilla Factory is a simple, yet enjoyable way to introduce the concept of production to your students. The book very simply explains the process of producing tortillas — from collecting the productive resources to marketing the final product. Students will learn the differences between the natural resources, capital resources, and human resources used in production.

Key Economic Concepts

Natural Resources	Productive Resources
Capital Resources	Human Resources
Human Capital	Investment
Interdependence	

Materials

Handouts 1 and 2	Classified Newspaper Ads
Magazines for cutting out pictures	

 ## Teaching Procedure

1. Read *The Tortilla Factory* orally to the class. Be sure to show all illustrations to the class as you read.

2. Write the words **Natural Resources**, **Human Resources**, and **Capital Resources** on the board. Before giving the definitions to the students, let them brainstorm what they think each concept might mean.

3. On the board, list each **productive resource** found in the book under the correct category.

4. Have each student choose three items from his or her desk (e.g., textbook, pencil, paper, ruler). Using Handout 1, have students list the specific **productive resources** necessary to produce the item.

5. Complete Handout 2, where students make a **human resource** collage. Provide the class with numerous magazines to use for cutting.

6. Complete Handout 3. Students must cut out different jobs from the classified advertisements, listing the necessary education/training and skills and estimating a yearly income/salary. You may want students to cut out more than three jobs. Discuss the handout questions.

Key Questions To Ask Students

1. What **production** steps are required to produce the tortillas? *(farmer using productive resources to grow corn, someone picking corn, truck taking corn to factory, machines grinding corn, etc.)*

2. What are the three basic **productive resources**? *(natural, human, capital)*

3. Can you produce tortillas without the use of **natural resources** (which are used to form raw materials) or **human resources**? Explain. *(No, you need both. You need raw materials to have something for human resources to process.)*

4. What **capital resources** are used to produce the tortillas? *(trucks, machines, buildings, etc.)* How do producers get capital goods? *(They must **save** — forgo buying consumption goods — and then **invest** the savings in capital goods. This requires discipline and risk-taking. There is no guarantee the investment will be profitable.)*

5. What special **human capital** *(skills, training, education)* do human resources need to produce tortillas? *(knowledge in growing corn, using capital resources, etc.)*

6. In the story, what are some examples of **interdependence** in the production of tortillas? *(depend on other producers to make tools and equipment, drive trucks, grind corn, have a grocery store to sell products, etc.)*

7. <u>Bonus Question</u>! What do the producers of tortillas have to do to make a **profit**? *(They have to receive a **price** that will cover the average cost to produce a tortilla.)*

 ## Follow-Up Activities

1. *Field Trip:* Go to a factory or workshop where unit production (one person making most of an entire product) is taking place.

2. *Assembly Line:* Design and produce a product using an assembly line. Write a paragraph describing the process. Put drawings and paragraphs on a bulletin board.

From Start to Finish

Product	Natural Resources (or Raw Materials)	Human Resources	Capital Resources

Choose one of the above items. Draw a sequence of pictures from start to finish showing how the product is made.

Human Resources

When you grow up, you will have to produce a good or a service. What education, training, and skills will you need?

Using clippings from magazines, make a collage of people (human resources) performing jobs. List the human capital (specialized education, training, and skills) necessary to do the work. Use other sheets of paper if necessary.

Picture of People Working (Human Resources)	**Necessary Human Capital** (Education, Skills, Training)

Classified Advertisements

NAME _____

Classified Advertisements (attach below)	Education, Training Requirements	Necessary Skills

1.

Yearly Income/Salary _____

2.

Yearly Income/Salary _____

3.

Yearly Income/Salary _____

Answer the questions below about the classified advertisements.

1. Which job pays the most? _____

   Which job pays the least? _____

2. Which job demands the most education and training? _____

   _____

3. What relationship do you see between the job salary and the required education/training

   and skills requirements? _____

   _____

4. What is the term economists use to describe the education, training, and skills that

   human resources have? _____

5. What **good** or **service** do *you* want to produce when you are an adult? _____

   _____

6. What education/training will you need? _____

   _____

   _____

7. What kinds of special **skills** will you need? _____

   _____

   _____

A Chair for My Mother
By Vera B. Williams

Summary

When all of their possessions were burned in a fire, a little girl and her mother and grandmother save all their extra money to buy a special chair. The characters make choices to save in order to obtain something important to them.

Key Economic Concepts

Human Resources	Wages
Savings	Consumers
Scarcity	Opportunity Cost

Materials

Handouts 1 and 2	3 x 5 Cards

 ## Teaching Procedure

1. Discuss decisions that people make concerning money. What do people do with their money? Write their responses on the board.

2. Read the story to the class.

3. Explain **human resources** and **wages**. Discuss "tips" and how they differ from wages. Form groups and have each group create a list of what students would save their tips for if they worked in a restaurant. Write the lists on large sheets of paper and display them in the room or hallway. Entitle the lists "Economic Wants We Would Save For."

4. Introduce the economic concepts of **scarcity** and **opportunity cost**.

5. Have each student draw and color a picture of a favorite good on a 3 x 5 card. Put cards on the board with masking tape. One at a time, have students identify their two best choices, choose the good they want, and identify the **opportunity cost**. (Lesson 4 in the *Play Dough Economics* Curriculum is a similar activity for teaching opportunity cost. See www.ncee.net)

6. Complete Handout 1.

7. Discuss family budgets. What goes into a budget? How are budgets helpful? Why are they difficult to keep? Organize students into groups of four and complete Handout 2 on budgeting. Have each group put its budget on a transparency when presenting to the class.

Key Questions To Ask Students

1. Explain the difference between a **producer** and a **consumer**. *(Producers make goods and services. Consumers purchase and use goods and services.)*

2. What are examples of **human resources** in the story? *(workers in diner, salespeople in store)* What do human resources receive for their labor? *(**wages** and **salaries**)*

3. What are examples of **scarcity** and **opportunity cost in** the story? *(Not enough income; choosing to save instead of buying other things, choosing one color of chair instead of another, etc.)*

4. What is the opportunity cost of **saving**? *(not being able to buy something you want in the present)* Which is more difficult – spending or saving? *(Saving is almost always more difficult!)* Why? *(It takes discipline to forgo current consumption.)*

5. What is the **opportunity cost** of spending? *(not saving for the future)*

 Follow-Up Activities

1. *Create a List:* Have students create a list of all the people and their responsibilities that make a diner successful.

2. *Field Trip:* Take a field trip to a local diner or restaurant.

3. *Speaker:* Invite a banker or another financial services provider to speak to the class about saving and investing.

4. *Classroom Jobs:* Create classroom jobs and pay students. Require them to save a percentage of their earnings and keep accurate records.

Opportunity Cost

1. Your aunt sent you $15 for your birthday. In the space below, draw, label, and color *two* goods (each with a price of $15) that you would like to buy with the money. Unfortunately, you can only buy one!

   What is your scarcity problem? _____

   Which good would you buy? _____

   What is your opportunity cost? _____

2. This is your lucky day! Your Uncle Joe sent you $20 for being a great kid. In the space below, draw, label, and color *three* goods, each with a price of $20, that you would like to buy.

   What is your scarcity problem? _____

   Which good would you buy? _____

   What is your opportunity cost? _____

3. If you decide to save the $20 your uncle sent you instead of spending it, do you still have an opportunity cost? Explain.

   What is your scarcity problem? _____

   Which good would you buy? _____

   What is your opportunity cost? _____

4. On the back, create some other opportunity cost situations/problems

Family Budgets

Pretend your group is a family of four. You must plan a monthly family budget with an after-tax income each month of $2,400. You must allocate money for the budget categories below. Make the best estimates you can. (You may need some grown-up advice!) When you are done, present your family budget to the class. How does your budget compare with the budget of the other groups? Does your teacher think it is a realistic budget? Show your budget to your parents and get their reaction.

Rent or House Payment

Food

Utilities (gas, electric, water, sewage, trash – estimate each)

Cable TV

Clothing Costs

Costs of Kids' Activities (Choose several.)

House Repairs

Car Repair Bills

Insurance (car, home, health)

Gasoline

Recreation (ball games, movies, etc.)

Eating Out

Presents (birthday, Christmas savings, wedding, etc.)

Other Expenses (stamps, kids' allowances, vacation savings fund, etc.)

Charitable Gifts/Religious Offerings

The Babe & I
By David A. Alder

Summary

The story is about a young boy growing up in New York during the Great Depression. He learns that his father is selling apples to support the family. The boy decides to help support the family by becoming a "newsie" — a street corner newspaper boy. He learns a great lesson about demand and market price — and also about the blessing of giving when Babe Ruth himself purchases a newspaper for $5.00, allowing the boy to see a Yankees game!

Key Economic Concepts

Demand/Supply	Income
Scarcity	Market Price
Profit	Money
Inflation	

Materials

Handouts 1 & 2	Construction Paper
Scissors	Glue
Crayons or colored pencils	

 ## Teaching Procedure

1. Introduce the story. Focus on the title. Have students discuss what the title might mean.

2. Give background information on the Great Depression.

3. Read the book. Discuss the economic concepts as they appear in the story.

4. Revisit the title. Discuss how the emphasis on Babe Ruth helped increase the **demand** for newspapers.

5. Discuss the Key Questions To Ask Students.

6. Do Handout 1, Designing Money. (Answer to question 6: Creating more money can not overcome scarcity. More money could just mean more **inflation**. To help overcome scarcity people need to produce more goods and services.)

7. Do Handout 2, Market Price Survey.

8. Based on the results of Handout 2, have the students write their observations in a multiple informational paragraph.

Key Questions To Ask Students

1. **Scarcity** is the condition of not being able to have all of the **goods** and **services** one wants. In the story, what was especially scarce? *(Because of the Depression, income was especially scarce because many people did not have jobs. In an economic sense, newspapers also were scarce. They were not free goods — they had a market price of two cents.)*

2. Why were **prices** and **wages** so low during the Great Depression? *(Demand for goods and services fell greatly, lowering prices. Businesses had to lay workers off or pay very low wages.)*

3. What job did the father actually have? How much did he earn? *(He sold apples for five cents each.)*

4. What job did the boy (narrator) find? What was the **market price** of the papers? *(He became a "newsie," selling newspapers for two cents each.)*

5. How much **profit** did the boy make on each newspaper? *(He purchased each paper for one cent so he made an accounting profit of one cent per paper.)*

6. What is **demand**? *(how much of something people will buy at different prices, holding other things constant)* How would a change in demand affect the selling of newspapers for the boys? *(The greater the demand, the more papers the boys could sell. Or, maybe they could have charged a higher price. If demand fell, they would sell less or could lower the price.)*

7. How did the boys increase the **demand** for their papers? *(They sold them near Yankee Stadium. They advertised by shouting how the papers would tell all about Babe Ruth.)*

8. Why did Babe Ruth pay more than the **market price** of two cents for the paper? *(He earned a large **income** and wanted to help the boys.)*

 Follow-Up Activities

1. Do Lessons 11 and 12, Market Price, in the *Play Dough Economics* curriculum. (See www.ncee.net.)
2. Have students create their own newspaper.
3. Conduct a school-wide survey on some topic of interest. Publish the results.
4. Write a report and give an oral presentation on a famous baseball player. Research the era in which he played.

Designing Money

People confront scarcity problems every day. The characters in the story faced a variety of scarcity problems, one being a limited amount of income. Imagine that the characters were given the opportunity to overcome scarcity by creating a new form of paper money. It is your job to help them develop this new paper money!

Using white construction paper, colored pencils, scissors, and glue, create an example of this new paper money. Make sure your money has the following characteristics of money: **scarce, portable, divisible, and durable**.

After you design your money, answer the questions below.

1. How did you make your currency difficult to counterfeit? In other words, how did you make it **scarce**?

2. Will you allow **checks** to be used as money? Explain.

3. Why did you choose this form of money?

4. How are you going to circulate your money?

5. What was difficult about creating a new kind of money?

6. Why would creating a new form of money <u>not</u> be the answer to overcoming scarcity in the real world?

Market Price Survey

Create five possible newspaper headings. Conduct a **survey** of your class to see which heading would get the students to purchase a newspaper.

Then, use the results to write a news story based on the best heading.

Headings   **Tally**

1._____

2._____

3._____

4._____

5._____

News Story

The Three Little Pigs
(Classic Nursery Tale)

Summary

Three little pigs are being threatened by a big, bad wolf. Each pig is forced to make a decision on how to protect himself from the wolf. What kind of house will each build?

Key Concepts

Natural Resources	Scarcity
Human Resources	Trade-Offs
Capital Resources	

Materials

Popsicle Sticks	Playing Cards
Legos	Classified Ads

Teaching Procedure

1. Prior to reading, introduce and define the key economic concepts found in the story.

2. Read the classic nursery tale, The Three Little Pigs, orally to the class.

3. After reading, brainstorm other alternative materials that could be used in the classroom to construct a model of each pig's home.

4. Divide class into three groups. Each member of group 1, group 2, and group 3 will construct a house representing straw, bricks, and sticks using playing cards for straw, Legos for bricks, and popsicle sticks for the stick house.

5. Test the durability of the construction by using a blow dryer or an electric fan to try to blow the house down. Have students write down their observations.

6. Use Handout 1, Brick, Wood, or Siding?, to have students research the advantages and disadvantages of using wood siding, vinyl siding, or brick to build a house. Explain to students that a choice to use one material involves **trading off** the benefits of using another.

7. Review the six parts of a business letter. Using Handout 2, have students write business letters to the Three Little Pigs and also to the Big Bad Wolf. (heading, date, inside address, salutation, body, closing) Important — have students include as many economic concepts as possible in their letters.

Key Questions To Ask Students

1. Why did each of the three little pigs have to build his own home? *(The family had a very limited amount of money, so Mother sent them out to make their own way in the world.)*

2. What **productive resources** were used to make the houses?
    *   Natural: straw, bricks, sticks
    *   Human: pigs (They acted like humans, though they were not really human!)
    *   Capital: hammer, saw, other tools, etc.

3. What **scarcity** situation did the three little pigs face when deciding how to build their houses? What did they choose? *(The pigs had to decide whether to use quick and cheaper materials or sturdy and more expensive materials.)*

4. What **trade-offs** did the pigs face when they made their house building decision? *(They traded-off the security of a sturdy brick house for the ease and low cost of building a house out of straw or sticks.)* What trade-offs do you face when deciding whether to purchase a small or large car? *(comfort and safety versus ease of handling, good gas mileage, etc.)*

5. What economic lesson did the pigs learn from this experience? *(It sometimes doesn't pay to choose the easy and inexpensive way to do something. It may be better to invest the time and resources to produce a more durable and sturdy item. In this story, that was certainly the case!)*

 Follow-Up Activities

1. Using play dough, make examples of a natural, capital, and human resource.

2. Read the book, *The 3 Little Pigs — The Wolf's Version,* to the class. Discuss or write how this version differs from the original.

3. Get copies of the play, *The Big Bad Wolf vs. The 3 Little Pigs,* published by the American Bar Association. (Go to www.abanet.org/publiced/mocktrials.html to order. Perform the play for a school audience. Have students design the scenery and costumes. One possibility is to make this a business project with the goal of making a profit. Go to http://www.19thcircuit-court.state.il.us/bkshelf/resource/mt_bbwolf.htm to view the play on the web.

4. Identify other examples of **trade-offs**. Discuss as a class. Write a paragraph about the trade-offs in a particular situation.

5. Read the following book to your students: *Babe: The Gallant Pig* (by Dick King-Smith), and also these nursery rhymes: Whose Little Pigs are These; Cobbler Cobbler; To Market, To Market; and This Little Piggy. Compare and contrast the pigs in these stories with The Three Little Pigs.

Brick, Wood, or Siding?

Directions:

1. Look in the "Houses for Sale" section of the newspaper. Cut out pictures of houses and glue them under the appropriate heading — wood siding, brick, or vinyl siding. Put the price under each picture.

2. Research these house building materials: wood, brick, and house siding. Explain how they are made, the characteristics of each, and the price. Then, complete the chart below, noting the advantages and disadvantages of using each material to build a house.

	Advantages	**Disadvantages**
Brick		
Wood Siding		
Vinyl Siding		

3. Write a paragraph entitled, "What I Would Use to Build a House." Make sure you carefully explain your choice!

Writing a Business Letter

Below, write a business letter to each or all of the pigs — and to the Big Bad Wolf. Explain why you think good or poor decisions were made. Be sure to include some economic concepts in your letter, such as natural resources, scarcity, and trade-offs. Also be sure to use the six basic parts of a business letter.

From the Mixed Up Files of Mrs. Basil E. Frankweiler
By E. L. Koningsburg

Summary

Eleven-year-old Claudia Kincaid feels that too much responsibility has been placed on her at home. To make her family appreciate her more, she decides to run away from home. Claudia persuades her younger brother, Jamie, to accompany her on a trip to a most unlikely place — the Metropolitan Museum of Art in New York City. (Chapter book)

Key Economic Concepts

Scarcity	Goods and Services
Savings	Opportunity Cost
Price	Interdependence
Inflation	

Materials

Handouts 1 & 2

Teaching Procedure

1. Before reading, give a brief background on the New York Metropolitan Museum of Art, including the location and the types of items on display. Ask students what kinds of things they would have to consider before running away to the Metropolitan Museum of Art.

2. Read *The Mixed Up Files of Mrs. Basil E. Frankweiler*. This book can be read two chapters at a time for a total of five reading days.

3. Define and discuss the key economic concepts. Tell students to point out examples of these concepts as you read.

4. After discussing the concepts, focus specifically on the concepts of **scarcity** and **opportunity cost**. Divide students into small groups and complete Handout 1. (The Decision Tree and Five-Step Models are in Part 3.)

5. Discuss the concept of **relative scarcity** (i.e., how the **price** of a good reflects how scarce it is relative to another good). Complete Handout 2.

Key Questions To Ask Students

1. What is the difference between a **good** and a **service**? What **services** did the children depend on to help make their escapade a success? *(school bus, train, museum, taxi, etc.)* This is an example of what economic concept? *(interdependence)*

2. What does the economics term **scarcity** mean? *(the condition of not being able to have all of the goods and services one wants)* How do we know a good or a service is scarce? *(It has a price.)* What was the children's most frequent scarcity problem? *(scarcity of money!)* What does scarcity always force us to do? *(make choices)*

3. How do we know if a good or service is **more scarce** than another? *(It has a higher price.)* What was the best example of a very scarce item in the story? *(angel statue of Michelangelo)* Why did it sell for only $225 in the auction? *(No one knew it was genuine, i.e., extremely scarce!)*

4. Compared to prices today, the prices of things in the story *(e.g., tuna sandwich - $ .35)* were very inexpensive. What is it called when the prices of almost all goods and services increase over time? *(**Inflation**)* What is the basic cause of **inflation**? *(too much money created relative to available goods and services)*

5. Claudia and Jamie made many choices. When Claudia chose to visit the U.N. instead of having dessert, what was her **opportunity cost**? *(dessert!)* What were other examples of opportunity cost in the story?

 Follow-Up Activities

1. *Video:* View the video *From the Mixed Up Files of Mrs. Basil E. Frankweiler.*

2. *Art Report*: Have students research and give an oral report on some of the art in the Metropolitan Museum of Art. What were some prices of the art pieces? Discuss why some art is very expensive and some isn't.

3. *Opportunity Cost Bulletin Board*: Display student descriptions and illustrations of a recent choice and the resulting **opportunity cost**.

4. *My Scarcity Situations*: Have students complete the My Scarcity Situations activity from Part 3 of this curriculum.

What Should I Take?

Fortunately, you're not running away from home like Claudia and Jamie! However, your best friend has invited you to go on a one-week backpacking trip in the Rocky Mountains. Your friend says you *must* take a sleeping bag, tent, canteen, mess kit, food, and a backpack. You want to take *many* extra things, including matches, extra clothes, maps, flashlight, extra flashlight batteries, knife, ax, aspirin, suntan lotion, mosquito repellant, poncho, books, first aid kit, compass, harmonica, collapsible fishing rod and gear, binoculars, and a book entitled *Surviving in the Wilderness*.

A. Unfortunately, you can only fit *nine* of these extra items in your backpack. In the blanks below list them *in your order of importance*.

1. _____   2. _____   3. _____

4. _____   5. _____   6. _____

7. _____   8. _____   9. _____

B. What is your **scarcity** problem? _____

C. What does scarcity force you to do? _____

D. When you make choices, there are alternatives you *do not choose*. When you chose your ninth item above, what was the best item you *did not* choose? _____
In economics, what do we call this best alternative? _____

E. Use the Decision Tree or the Five-Step Decision Grid to show why you chose item 9 above instead of the next best item.

Scarce and More Scarce!

In economics, any good or service that has a price is considered scarce. However, some goods and services are **more scarce** than others. For example, a pencil is considered a scarce good since it is not freely available and has a price. It is not as scarce, however, as a gold necklace. The more scarce something is, the higher the price.

Sometimes events occur that change the scarcity of certain goods or services. Read each scenario below and answer the questions.

1. A snow storm with record snowfall suddenly hit Indiana in late October. What goods or services might become much more scarce? Why?

2. Your geographical region has been hit with a record heat wave. Record high temperatures are expected for the next several days. What goods and services might become more scarce? Would their price rise? Explain why or why not.

3. Draw a cartoon strip illustrating a situation in which the relative scarcity of a good or service changes (for example, see 1. and 2. above).

The Sign of the Beaver
by Elizabeth George Speare

Summary

Matt and his father have traveled to the Maine wilderness to start a new settlement for their family. He and his father build a comfortable cabin. His father returns to the city to get the family and leaves Matt alone to protect the family cabin. Matt is befriended by an Indian clan leader and his grandson, who teach him how to survive alone in the wilderness. In return, Matt teaches the grandson English and, in the process, develops a close friendship with the Indian boy. (Chapter book)

Key Economic Concepts

natural resources	barter
scarcity	trade
opportunity cost	interdependence

Materials

Handout 1 — Making a Log Cabin
Handout 2 — Decisions, Decisions, Decisions
Handout 3 — Scarcity Drawing
Handout 4 — What Will Matt Do?

Teaching Procedure

1. Before reading the story, review definitions of the economic concepts that will be found in *The Sign of the Beaver.*

2. Read the story together, a few chapters at a time. Have students identify economic concepts as they appear in the story.

3. Discuss the **natural resources** that were needed by settlers to build their homes in the wilderness. Also discuss the concepts of **scarcity** and **opportunity cost,** giving examples.

4. Assign each student the task of constructing a model of a log cabin that might have been built by early settlers. Use Handout 1, Making a Log Cabin.

5. Have students complete Handout 2, Decisions, Decisions, Decisions!, using a situation from the story.

6. Scarcity Drawing — Activity 3. Have students think of a situation illustrating a **scarcity** of goods or services. Have students illustrate this situation. Make a bulletin board displaying their work.

7. At the end of the story, Matt is faced with a major decision. Should he move with the Beaver tribe or should he stay with his cabin? Have students complete Handout 4.

Key Questions To Ask Students

1. What were some of the **natural resources** that Matt and his father used to build their house? *(trees, mud for chinking, etc.)*

2. After Ben left and after the confrontation with the bear, Matt was faced with an even greater **scarcity** of what items? Discuss. *(molasses, flour, rifle)*

3. What does **barter** mean? *(exchanging goods or services without money)*
   Who benefits when people barter/trade? *(both parties in the trade)*

4. What barter agreement did Attean's grandfather make with Matt? *(Attean would teach Matt to survive if Matt taught Attean to speak and read English)*

5 Why don't people barter much today? *(Bartering is inefficient. Each person must want what the other person has and be willing to trade.)* What do people use to make barter/trade more efficient? *(money!)*

6. What is **interdependence**? *(Interdependence occurs when people and nations depend on one another to provide each other's economic wants)*. What was an example of interdependence in the story? *(Attean provided Matt with food and knowledge how to survive. Matt provided Attean with English lessons.)*

7. What is **opportunity cost?** *(the value of your best alternative when you make a choice.)* Give an example of opportunity cost from the story. *(Matt's father had to give up the chance to stay with Matt when he went to get his family, etc.)*

 Follow-Up Activities

1. Do *Play-Dough Economics* Lesson 6: *"Trade — Getting the Things We Want."* (See www.ncee.net)

2. Research various Indian tribes to find out what items they usually used for trading.

Making A Log Cabin

Project Requirements:

1. Have each student (or small groups of students) build a model of a pioneer cabin. The project should be done outside of class. The work time to complete the project should be about 2-3 weeks. Encourage students to work with their parents or another adult.

Follow these directions and suggestions:

- Plot of Land: Suggested materials could be real grass, dirt, or modeling clay.

- Foliage: On the plot of land place trees, shrubs, flowers, fallen branches. etc.

- Roof: Roof must be removable to expose the inside of the cabin. Suggested materials are popsicle sticks, tongue depressors, etc.

- Chinking Material: Logs must have chinking material between them. Students can use clay, flour and water paste, etc.

- Furniture: The inside of cabin should be furnished according to the description given in the story.

- Fireplace and Door: The cabin must contain a fireplace and at least one door.

2. As part of the cabin display, have students list all of the **natural resources** and **capital resources** used to make a real pioneer cabin.

3. Language Arts Assignment: Have students write a short paper describing the steps involved in building a model cabin.

4. (Optional) Have students make a presentation on how they built their cabin. Upper elementary students could create a PowerPoint presentation.

Decisions, Decisions, Decisions!

The characters in many stories have to solve **scarcity** problems, and this usually means having to make some difficult decisions! Answer the questions below about a scarcity problem that someone in the story had to solve.

1. What was a **scarcity problem** confronted by one of the book's characters?

   _____

2. What were the **alternatives** (choices) for solving the problem?

   _____

   _____

3. What **decision** did the character make?

   _____

4. What was the **opportunity cost** of the decision?

   _____

5. Write a paragraph explaining why you think it was a good or bad decision. Write neatly and use correct spelling and grammar.

Scarcity Drawing

There are several examples of scarcity situations in the story. Draw a picture of a scarcity situation/problem. At the bottom of the page, write several complete sentences explaining your picture.

Describe your picture using complete sentences.

Does *everyone* experience scarcity, even rich people? Explain.

What Will Matt Do?

Matt is faced with making a major decision — to go or not to go with the Beaver tribe. Complete the following chart, then explain why Matt should stay or go. Identify what he would gain and his opportunity cost in both decisions.

To Go (What he would gain by going)	Opportunity Cost (What he would give up by going)

To Stay (What he would gain by staying)	Opportunity Cost (What he would give up by staying)

Now write, neatly, and in paragraph form, what you think Matt should do and why. Be sure to use complete sentences.

What Matt Should Do

Stone Fox
by John Reynolds Gardiner

Summary

Ten-year-old Little Willy faces a big job when his grandfather falls ill. It is up to him to save their potato farm from the tax collectors. Willy has a big economic problem — he needs five hundred dollars to pay his grandfather's back property **taxes**. When Willy sees a poster announcing a $500 prize for the National Dogsled Race, he decides to enter the race. But other people want to run the race, too, including Stone Fox, who has never lost a race! (Chapter book)

Key Economic Concepts:

Taxes   Scarcity
Specialization   Opportunity Cost
Capital Resources

Materials: Handouts: Taxes and You; Decisions, Decisions;
                            Writer's Journal; Economics Review Test

 Teaching Procedure

1. Carefully read and discuss this story with your students. Discuss the variety of problems that faced Little Willy.

2. Explain the term **property tax**. Discuss why taxes were a big problem for Willy.

3. Define and explain the economic concepts of **scarcity** and **opportunity cost.** Ask students to list some of the **scarcity** problems that affected Little Willy. *(scarcity of money to pay the taxes and the race entrance fee, having only one dog to pull his sled during the race, time to harvest the potato crop, no horse to use to harvest potatoes, etc.)* What was the **opportunity cost** of Willy using his $50 savings to enter the race? *(giving up using the savings for college).*

4. Explain the economic concepts of **services** and **specialization**. Ask students to list examples of specialization in the story. *(banker, potato farmer, tax collector, doctor, store keeper, dogsled racer, mayor)* Discuss the types of goods or services each of these provides.

5. Homework assignment: Have students complete the Taxes and You worksheet as a "family" assignment.

6. Use the Decisions, Decisions worksheet to identify the decision that was made and the results. *(Answers: 1. Decision — Grandfather decided not to pay taxes. Result — He owed $500 in back taxes and suffered poor health from stress and worry. 2. Decision — Willy had to harvest the potato crop. Result/Opportunity Cost — He wasn't able to do other things during that time, e.g. play, swim, other chores. 3. Decision — Willy used his*

$50 savings to enter the race. Result/Opportunity Cost — He wasn't able to use the money for other things, especially college. 4. Decision — Willy decided to use Searchlight alone to pull the sled. Result/Opportunity Cost — Searchlight dies of heart failure/exhaustion. 5. Decision — Stone Fox lets Willy win the race. Result/Opportunity Cost — He gives up the chance to win the prize.)

7. Have students complete the Writer's Response Journal.

8. Give students the Stone Fox Economics Review Test.

 Key Questions To Ask Students

1. What kind of farm did Grandfather own? *(potato farm)* What major **scarcity** problem did grandfather face? *(He had too many expenses and not enough income from potato farming to pay his **taxes**.)*

2. What are **capital resources**? *(tools, equipment, machinery, buildings, etc.)* What **capital resources** do you think Willy and his grandfather would need to produce potatoes? *(plow, work animals, baskets, barn, truck, etc.)*

3. What are different kinds of **taxes** paid by consumers and producers? *(income, sales, property, excise, Social Security, etc.)* What kind of tax did Grandfather owe? *(property tax)*

4. Why do people pay taxes? *(so government can provide goods and services)* How is tax money used? *(Establish Legal Framework/Civic Protection: police, fire, court system, national defense, etc. Provide Other Services: education, snow plows, public transportation, libraries, roads, bridges, lighthouses, etc. Income Distribution: Social Security, food stamps, public medical clinics, etc.*

4. What is **specialization?** *(People specialize when they work in jobs where they produce a few special goods or services.)* When people specialize, they often focus on what they enjoy or do best. People also usually get specialized education or training. What are specialized jobs in your community? What skills are needed to succeed in each? *(e.g. Doctor — very high levels of education and training are needed. Auto mechanic — no minimum education is always needed, but need high skill levels which often come from technical courses. Teacher — college degree is necessary and continuous education is required after that.)*

5. Why does **scarcity** force people to choose among alternatives? *(People can't have everything they want — there aren't enough productive resources/money/time. See 3. in Teaching Procedure for scarcity examples in the story.)*

6. Every decision has an **opportunity cost**. What is opportunity cost? *(When making a decision, it is the value of the best alternative given up.)* Explain why every decision has an opportunity cost. *(There is always an alternative choice that is given up.)*

7. When Stone Fox let Willy win the race, what was the opportunity cost of that decision? *(Stone Fox gave up the opportunity to win the race, along with the $500.)* Do you think that Stone Fox was happy with his decision? *(yes)*

 Follow-Up Activities

1. Watch the "Stone Fox" video with your students. Have students make a "compare and contrast" chart showing how alike and how different the book is from the movie.

2. Have students research and write a short report on one of the following topics: National Dogsled Races; Jackson Hole, Wyoming; Shoshone Indian tribe; potato farming; or Samoyed dogs; dogsleds, etc.

3. Have students research the history of **taxes**. What are early examples of taxation? Who receives tax money? How is tax money collected and used?

4. Bring in some potatoes and discuss the variety of ways people eat potatoes. (mashed, fried, baked, boiled, potato pancakes, etc.) For extra credit, have students bring samples of their favorite potato dish to share with the class. Make a potato recipe book to send home with students.

5. Art Connection: Make potato print pictures or potato print wrapping paper using colored ink or paint and cut potato halves.

6. Science Connection: Grow regular and sweet potatoes in a jar and discuss the parts of a potato *(vegetable, eye, peel, roots, etc.)* Discuss the importance of water cycle, soil, fertilizer, seasons, etc. for growing and harvesting successful potato crops.

7. Consumer Science: Discuss the various types and varieties of potatoes. What is the approximate price of a 5 lb. bag of potatoes? Discuss why the price constantly changes. *(supply and demand)*

Taxes & You

Name _____ Date _____

What are benefits that people get from **taxes**? With a family member, read through the statements below. Check yes or no for each statement.

	Yes	No
1. A family member works for the government.	_____	_____
2. Children in your family attend a public school.	_____	_____
3. Someone in your family has a library card.	_____	_____
4. Children in your family ride on a public school bus.	_____	_____
5. Members of your family drive on roads & highways.	_____	_____
6. Members of your family have used a public park.	_____	_____
7. Someone in your family has used the 911 telephone number.	_____	_____
8. You have a fire department located in your community.	_____	_____
9. You have a police department in your community.	_____	_____
10. A snow plow plowed a road near your house or school.	_____	_____
11. A member of your family has played on a public playground.	_____	_____
12. Your school offers "free" or reduced school lunches.	_____	_____
13. Someone in your community has been treated for an illness at a "free" medical clinic.	_____	_____
14. Some people in your community receive "Food Stamps."	_____	_____
Total	_____	_____

Write a sentence explaining where the **services** above come from? _____

_____

_____

_____

Are government services "**scarce**?" Explain. _____

_____

_____

Decisions, Decisions!

People in the story had a variety of decisions to make. Identify the decision made in response to the problem and then identify the **result** or **opportunity cost** of the decision.

Problem	Decision	Result/ Opportunity Cost
1. For years, Grandfather needed money to pay property taxes on the farm.		
2. Grandfather was sick and couldn't harvest the potato crop.		
3. Little Willy needed $50 to register for the National Dogsled Race.		
4. Little Willy didn't have a team of dogs for the race.		
5. Stone Fox can win the race or let Little Willy win.		

Writer's Response Journal

Name: _____ Date:_____

1. Why did Little Willy need $500? _____
_____
_____

2. What was wrong with Grandfather? _____
_____
_____

3. Why were the tax collectors after Grandfather?
_____
_____
_____

4. What was the relationship between Little Willy and Searchlight?
_____
_____
_____

5. How did Stone Fox treat Little Willy when they first met?
_____
_____

6. What happened to Searchlight at the end of the race?
_____
_____

7. Why did Stone Fox let Little Willy win the race?
_____
_____
_____

8. How do you think Grandfather felt when Little Willy won the race and paid off the property tax?
_____
_____
_____

Stone Fox Economics Review Test

Name _____

1. Grandfather **specialized** in _____ farming.

2. List three **human resources** found in this story and their area of specialization.
   1. _____
   2. _____
   3. _____

3. List three **scarcity** problems/situations found in this story.
   1. _____
   2. _____
   3. _____

4. List two **capital resources** needed to harvest the potato crop.
   1. _____
   2. _____

5. What is **opportunity cost?** _____

   _____

   Give an example of opportunity cost in the story. _____

   _____

   _____

6. What are **taxes**? _____

   _____

   What kind of taxes did grandfather need to pay? _____

7. Write a sentence explaining what would happen if Grandfather did not pay his taxes.

   _____

   _____

8. List three things that are paid for with taxes.
   1. _____
   2. _____
   3. _____

Holes
By Louis Sachar

Summary

Stanley Yelnats is under a curse begun by his "pig-stealing" great-great-grandfather years ago. Stanley finds himself in a detention camp for boys, where he was sent — unjustly — for stealing a pair of sneakers. Every day, each boy must learn character by digging a perfectly round hole — five feet wide and five feet deep — in the bottom of dried-up Camp Green Lake. Stanley soon realizes that the warden has other reasons besides character for digging the holes! But what could be buried under a dried-up lake? (Chapter book)

Key Economic Concepts

Scarcity   Opportunity Cost
Natural Resources   Entrepreneur

Materials

Construction Paper   Art Supplies
Handouts 1 and 2   Video Equipment

 ## Teaching Procedure

1. Discuss the economic concept of **natural resources**. (To help teach this concept and 21 others, try using lessons from the KidsEcon Posters© curriculum. See kidseconposters.com.)

2. Read Chapter 1. Then divide the class into small groups. Have each group create a list of natural resources mentioned in Chapter 1. Discuss the different lists.

3. Discuss the concept of **scarcity**. Read Chapters 2-6. Have the students find the sentence in Chapter 6 that mentions scarcity. Then have students complete Handout 1, Scarce and More Scarce! They must write a paragraph discussing the sentence. *(Handout answers: 1. At a zero price, if there is not enough for everyone to have all they want, it is considered scarce. That is, it is not freely available to everyone who wants it. 2. If it has a price, it is considered scarce. 3. saltwater at the beach, sand in the desert 4. The more scarce it is, the higher the price.)*

4. Discuss **opportunity cost.** Do Handout 2, Opportunity Cost.

5. Read Chapters 7-49. Discuss the concept, **entrepreneur**. Then read chapter 50.

6. Create a new product. Make a poster advertising your product. Write a well-written paragraph explaining why people should purchase your product.

Key Questions To Ask Students

1. The environment of Camp Green Lake was very harsh. What **natural resource** was very scarce? *(water/rain)*. Why? *(Legend says that when Sam and Mary Lou were killed and the school burned, the lake dried up and no rain fell.)* Is water in your home scarce? *(Yes, but not as scarce as the water at Camp Green Lake! This is why the water in your home has a relatively low price.)*

2. Besides water, what is the other **scarce** item that was a major part of the story? *(Clyde Livingston's shoes)*. Explain why these shoes were scarce. *(He was a star player — only one of a kind!)*

3. How did the **scarcity** of the shoes affect their value? *(Because they were very scarce, they would command a high price at the auction.)*

4. When we make a choice, there is always an **opportunity cost**. *(the value of our best alternative choice)* Stanley made many choices throughout the story. Name two and discuss the opportunity cost of each decision. *(Answers will vary.)*

5. Stanley's father was willing to take the **risk** of experiencing a loss (or earning a profit) by looking for ways to make new things. What is the economics term used to describe someone like Mr. Yelnats? *(entrepreneur)* Are **entrepreneurs** usually successful? *(Not always! Only about 50% of businesses are still operating after the first three years. Starting and running a successful new business is very difficult! It requires much work and perseverance.)*

6. At the end of the story, Mr. Yelnats is successful. Explain how he is successful and how Clyde Livingston helps. *(Mr. Yelnats creates no-smell sneakers and Clyde advertises the new product.)*

 Follow-up Activities

1. Write a new ending to the story. Include three different economic concepts.

2. Based on the product you created in step six of the teaching procedure, make and present a commercial for your product.

3. Have a sports figure come and talk to your class. Have him or her focus on product endorsement.

4. Draw and color a picture of what you think Camp Green lake looked like before and after Sam was killed.

Scarce and More Scarce!

In the second paragraph of Chapter 6, it says, "Because of the scarcity of water, each camper was only allowed a four-minute shower." Answer the questions below about the important concept of **scarcity**.

1. In economics, what does it mean if something is "scarce?"

   _____

   _____

2. How do we know if something is a "scarce" good or service?

   _____

   _____

3. Circle the things below which typically are *not* considered scarce?

   Gold   Tickets to an Indianapolis Colts game   Saltwater at the beach

       Water in your home   Water in the desert   Sand in the desert

4. In economics, how can we tell if something is scarce or not very scarce?

   _____

5. Write a paragraph describing the scarcity sentence above from Chapter 6. Make sure you give a good explanation of scarcity!

Opportunity Cost

In the story, there were many examples of **opportunity cost**. At one point, Stanley found a gold tube. He knew that if he gave it to the warden, he would get a day off. He also knew that if he let X-Ray have it, he would stay in the good graces of the guys.

1. On the back or on a separate piece of paper, carefully write a paragraph explaining Stanley's situation with the gold tube and what he decided to do. Then answer the following questions.

2. In the situation of the gold tube, what were Stanley's two choices?

3. When he made a decision, what was his opportunity cost?

4. Why do you think Stanley made the choice he did? Do you think it was a good choice? Explain.

5. What choice would *you* have made? Why?

Lunch Money
by Andrew Clements

Summary

Greg is a sixth grader with a love for money. He had his first lemonade stand in second grade and is always looking for new ways to make money. Greg recently discovered that most students bring extra money to school each day, so he has decided it's the best place to make his fortune. (Chapter book)

Economic Concepts

Entrepreneur	Saving/Investing
Competition	Price
Capital Resources	Insurance
Advertising	Profit
Specialization	Human capital

Materials

Handouts 1-5

Teaching Procedure

1. Before reading the book, discuss what students do with the extra change they may have in their pockets. Do they spend it or do they save it?

2. Discuss the different types of items that students would buy with their "pocket change." Write examples on the board.

3. Next introduce students to the economic concepts that will be found in the story. Write them on the board and review their definitions.

4. Read *Lunch Money* orally to the class or individually if copies are available. Point out and discuss economic concepts as you read.

5. Following the completion of the book, have students complete Handout 1, Economic Concepts in the Story. (To review concepts, see definitions in Part 1.)

6. Discuss **profit**. Go over the definition of profit: Sales Revenues - All the Costs of Production. Remind students that the major cost of production of Greg's comics was his time — but that he did *not* include this in his production costs. This was why his accounting profit, per comic, was so high. To get a more accurate understanding of profit, students must realize that there is an **opportunity cost** to the entrepreneur's time. Greg or Maura could be doing other valuable things with their time.

7. Have students complete Handout 2, The Comic Business — Costs and Profit. *(Answers: 1. a. $4.60, b. $6.21, c. $8.96 2. He did not include the value of his time. This is very important. He could be doing other valuable things with his limited time. 3. a. $3.45 +$1.15 = $4.60 b. $4.14 + $1.38 = $5.52)*

8. Greg was fascinated by **money**, and, indeed, money has always been a topic of interest to many people! Have students complete Handout 3, Money Sayings. Then discuss as a class.

9. A key to being a successful **entrepreneur** is looking for and recognizing *opportunities* around you — opportunities to help consumers solve problems, satisfy unmet wants, or improve their lives. Give students Handout 4, Starting My Own Business, in which they create their own business ideas and plans. Encourage them to get advice from their parents or other family members. Let students present their business ideas to the class. Encourage students to implement their business.

10. Discuss the things that Greg wanted to buy if he had all the money in the world. Then assign Handout 5, a composition entitled "If I Had All the Money in the World, What Would I Do With It?"

 Key Questions To Ask Students

1. What was the most important thing in the world to Greg Kenton? *(money)* Was this a good or bad thing? *(It was good in that it motivated Greg to be productive and not waste his time. It was bad in that it dominated all his thinking and actions.)*

2. What is an **entrepreneur?** *(someone who takes the risk of experiencing a loss or earning a profit by starting or expanding a business.)* In what ways was Greg an entrepreneur? *(He was always looking for <u>opportunities</u>! At home, he did his brother's chores, kept the deposit funds from the recycling, shined his dad's shoes, dug up dandelions, cleaned the scuff marks off the kitchen tile, and sold lemonade. At school, he sold candy, gum, miniature toys, and comics.)*

3. What is **human capital?** *(the education, skills, and abilities a person has)* What human capital did Greg and Maura have? Why was this important to their business? *(Greg and Maura had artistic, organizational, and entrepreneurial skills. These were important in order to produce comic books and make a profit.)*

4. Who was initially in **competition** with Greg? *(Maura)* In the business world, why is competition usually good? *(It forces businesses to produce very efficiently so they can keep their prices competitive with other businesses. This usually leads to higher quality goods and services.)*

5. Who eventually became Greg's business partner? *(Maura!)* What is **profit**? *(Profit is the money remaining after subtracting all the costs of production from sales revenues. In Chapter 4, what were Greg's costs of production to produce his Chunky comics himself? ($.02 per comic, for ink, paper, and two staples.)*

6. What productive resource is *not* counted when Greg computes his profit? *(his own time/labor)* Is this omission important? *(Yes! It takes a lot of time to draw and produce the comics. There is an opportunity cost to this time – Greg could be doing other valuable things.)*

7. In Chapter 14, Greg decides to go into business with Maura even though she demanded 75% of any profits made from her own books. Why did Greg agree to this? *(He knew she would figure out how to make and sell the books herself. At least he would make 25% off her work.)*

8. Was their book business successful in making a profit? *(Yes, in the end they had a thriving business, sold a lot of books, and made a profit.)*

 Follow-Up Activities

1. As a class, open up a restaurant during your normal lunch time. Turn your classroom into the restaurant of your choice. Choose a restaurant name, come up with a menu, make placemats and centerpieces, and invite another class to dine in your restaurant. Students can be the servers; parents should help prepare the meal. Decorate the class in the theme of your restaurant. (Italian, Mexican, etc.) This is a really worthwhile and fun activity for you and your students. (Take plenty of pictures and contact the local media!)

2. Make a bulletin board displaying pictures of your restaurant.

3. Cartoon Strip: Have students make up a 6 to 8 frame comic strip exhibiting any one of the economic concepts found in the story.

4. Have students work with a partner to create a good to sell at a store. Set a day aside for another classroom to come in and buy the items using "monopoly type" money. Then discuss what sold the best and why.

5. Encourage students to start their own real businesses: pet sitting, lawn mowing, baby sitting, painting, etc.

Economic Concepts in the Story

There are many economic concepts illustrated in *Lunch Money*. Define each concept below and identify an example of it in the story.

1. Entrepreneur

2. Competition

3. Capital Resources

4. Human Capital

5. Specialization

6. Price

7. Advertising

8. Profit

9. Saving/Investing

The Comic Business — Costs and Profit

Name _____

1. Below are examples of Greg's sales and costs from selling his Chunky Comics. Compute Greg's profit. (Profit = Sales Revenues – All Production Costs)

a. Price – $.25
   Sales – 20 comics
   Costs – $.02 each

b. Price – $.25
   Sales – 27 comics
   Costs – $.02 each

c. Price – $.30
   Sales – 32 comics
   Costs – $.02 each

Profit = _____   **Profit =** _____   **Profit =** _____

2. What is one major cost Greg did *not* include in 1. above? _____
   Why is this important? _____
   _____

3. When Maura joined the business, she insisted on receiving 75% (3/4) of the profits on the books *she* created. Given this fact, compute Greg's profit.

a. Price – $.25
   Sales (Greg's comics) – 15
   Sales (Maura's comics) – 20
   Production Costs – $.02

b. Price – $.25
   Sales (Greg's comics) – 18
   Sales (Maura's comics) – 24
   Production Costs – $.02

Profit = _____   **Profit =** _____

4. On the back, use the concept of <u>opportunity cost</u> to explain whether you think it was a good decision for Greg and Maura to produce and sell comic books.

Money Sayings

Directions: Greg loved money — as do a lot of people! Write the meaning of the "money sayings" below. Then, find *other* money sayings and write down their authors and meanings, too. (Ask your parents for help or do an Internet search!)

"A penny saved is a penny earned."   Benjamin Franklin

_____

_____

"Remember that time is money."   Benjamin Franklin

_____

_____

"Lack of money is not an obstacle; lack of an idea is an obstacle!"   Ken Hakuta

_____

_____

"How much better it is to get wisdom than gold!"   Bible — Proverbs 16:16

_____

_____

"A man is usually more careful about his money than his principles."   Oliver Wendell Holmes

_____

_____

"You can't get rid of poverty by giving people money."   P. J. O'Rourke

_____

_____

"Wealth consists in not having great possessions, but in having few wants."   Epicurus

_____

_____

"Money made through dishonest practices will not last long."   Chinese proverb

_____

_____

"Money talks, but all it ever says is goodbye."   Unknown

_____

_____

Note: This lesson was taken from *Pint-Size Economics: Economics and Personal Finance for Kids*, Indiana Council for Economic Education, 2006. Available at www.kidseconposters.com. Used with permission.

Starting My Own Business

Greg was always looking for an opportunity to make money. That's what entrepreneurs do — they look for opportunities to provide consumers with goods or services that will help them solve problems, satisfy unmet wants, or improve their lives. Entrepreneurs calculate what productive resources they will need to provide the good or service. Then they put a plan of action together and start the business. It takes a lot of work, but it may be worth it!

Could *you* be an entrepreneur? Think of a business you could start in your neighborhood. Follow the steps below and plan your own business! Use other paper if necessary.

1. What **opportunities** can you see to help consumers solve a problem, satisfy an unmet need, or improve their lives? What **good** or **service** could you provide?

2. What **competition** is there for your idea/business? Are other people or businesses providing the same or similar goods or services? Will you be able to compete?

3. What **productive resources** will you need to begin your business? How will you get them? Can you afford them?

4. Is there much **risk** in starting your business? Do you have enough time to start and run the business? What is the **opportunity cost** of your time?

5. How much **profit** do you think you could make with your business? Is it worth the risk?

If I Had All the Money in the World...

Write a composition entitled, "If I Had All the Money in the World, What Would I Do With It?" Would you spend it, save it, give it away...?

If I Had All the Money in the World, What Would I Do With It?

Island of the Blue Dolphin
By Scott O'Dell

Summary

Karana is an Indian girl stranded alone on an island for 18 years. When the rest of her tribe is forced to flee the island, she learns to use her human resources and the island's natural resources to survive. (Chapter book)

Key Economic Concepts

Natural Resources	Human Resources
Scarcity	Capital Resources
Trade	Specialization
Division of Labor	Conservation

Materials

Handouts 1, 2, and 3
Five-Step Decision Grid
   (in Part 3)

 ## Teaching Procedure

1. Introduce the story to your students. Discuss these questions:
   a. What is a desert island?
   b. How could you survive on a desert island?
   c. What kinds of **productive resources** would there be on the island?

2. Introduce the concept of **scarcity**. What **natural resources** would be scarce on a desert island? What natural resources would *not* be scarce there? (sea water, air)

   Note: Some students might think that the natural resources on the island were not scarce since they were freely available to Karana. It is true that some, like the air and sea water, were not scarce. But the other resources were indeed scarce for Karana, even though they had no market price, since it took her limited time and energy to get them!

3. Discuss with the students the different types of **productive resources**.

4. Read the story. It might be best to divide the book into sections. (Chapters 1-5, 6-10, 11-15, 16-20, 21-29) After each section, be sure to discuss any pertinent economic concepts.

5. As the students read the book, have them keep a journal focusing on how Karana uses the resources to survive.

6. Complete Handouts 1, 2, and 3.

7. Divide into small groups. Have students complete the responses and then use the Five-Step Decision Model to analyze the elephant conservation scenario. The scenario is based on actual policies being debated in Africa.

 Key Questions To Ask Students

1. How did tribe members **specialize** in **production**? *(There are various examples. The men and women had special, strictly defined tasks within the tribe.)*

2. What did the Aleuts want to **trade** for the right to hunt otter? *(They agreed to divide the catch.)* Who benefits when a voluntary trade is made — and promises are kept? *(Both parties expect to benefit.)*

3. What effect did the Aleuts' hunting have on the otters? *(They hunted too many, threatening the natural balance; otters became more scarce.)*

4. Why is it difficult to **conserve** natural resources such as water and wild animals? *(When no one owns natural resources there is less incentive to conserve. No one owned the otters. So they were over-hunted.)*

5. Did Karana have to be a **producer** to survive? *(Yes!)*

6. How were Karana's **productive resources** different from those used by producers in your community? *(many differences in all three productive resource categories)*

7. The island's **natural resources** were very important to Karana. How were these resources used? *(build a shelter, find food, safety and security, etc.)* What natural resources were especially **scarce**? *(wood, elephant teeth)*

 Follow-Up Activities

1. *Flash Cards:* Make flash cards with the name of a resource on one side and the type of resource on the other.

   Examples: Water (front)   Natural Resource (back)
                 Hammer (front)   Capital Resource (back)

2. *Keep a Diary*: Create a diary based on Karana's daily activities. Highlight every entry that deals with productive resources.

3. *Vocabulary List*: Keep a vocabulary list of all economic concepts discussed.

4. *Build a Shelter:* Provide a limited supply of materials. (glue, popsicle sticks, yarn, construction paper, wood chips, etc.) Have the students use these materials to build some kind of a shelter. Have them explain what human resources they used to construct the shelter.

5. *Deer Conservation Plan:* Create a conservation plan to help control the deer population in Indiana. Ask someone from the Indiana Department of Natural Resources to speak to the class about this problem. Or, research this very real problem on the Internet. Report the findings to the class.

Natural Resources and Scarcity

1. List the **natural resources** mentioned in the story and how Karana used them.

   <u>Natural Resource</u>   <u>How Used</u>

2. What does the economic term **scarcity** mean? Give an example.

3. Since the natural resources on the island were freely available to Karana, how could they possibly be considered **scarce**?

4. Which of these resources was the **most scarce** for Karana? Why?

5. Which natural resources in the story could actually be considered "free" to Karana, i.e., *not* scarce? Explain.

Jobs and Special Skills

1. What does **division of labor** mean? Give an example.

2. How was the labor divided in the Indian village? How is the labor divided in your school? Give examples.

3. What special skills (**human capital**) helped Karana to survive?

4. Write a paragraph describing the good or service you want to produce when you grow up. Tell why. Also describe the education, skills, and training it will take. How will you get the education, skills, and training?

....

What I Want to Produce When I Grow Up

Conservation and Stewardship

1. What does it mean to be a good **steward** of natural resources? Do you think Karana was a good steward? Why?

2. In some places, certain wild animal species are threatened and some have become extinct. Which animal in the story was threatened? _____

   Why? _____

3. Why is a wild animal like the otter or eagle threatened, while an animal like the chicken is not?

4. Use the Five-Step Decision Model to solve this conservation problem.

   Scenario: *Kumutu is a poor village in Zimbabwe. The village lies next to a large game preserve. Unfortunately, wild elephants roam on village lands, often damaging crops. The villagers want to be able to kill some elephants for food and for crop protection. Villagers can also make a lot of money from selling the ivory tusks and from selling hunting permits each year to safari operators. The money will greatly improve the villagers' difficult lives. However, at this time there is a total ban on killing elephants.*

   To help the villagers, the government has proposed an Elephant Conservation Plan. It would give villagers permits to kill three elephants each year or to sell the hunting rights for these three elephants to safari operators. According to a government spokesman, "There is a surplus of elephants in the park now and this would give villagers a way to protect their crops and improve their lives. Also, the villagers would be motivated to watch out for poachers on their land. The poachers are killing many elephants and the government just doesn't have enough money to stop them."

   "This plan is awful!" replied Sally Jones from the Animal Humane Society. "An elephant is not a cow. There are other ways to help villagers besides killing these beautiful animals!" Should the Conservation Plan be implemented?

Beetles Lightly Toasted
By Phyllis Reynolds Naylor

Summary

The subject of this year's contest at school is "Conservation." Ten-year-old Andy Moller lives on an Iowa farm and he and his cousin, Jack, are both determined to win the $50 prize. The two boys devise hilarious ways to conserve resources — including eating insects and cooking hamburgers on a car engine! (Chapter book)

Key Economic Concepts

Productive Resources   Scarcity
Boycott   Price
Role of Government   Productivity
Conservation

Materials

Handouts 1 and 2

Teaching Procedure

1. List and discuss the key economic concepts. Have the students write the definitions of these concepts.

2. Introduce the book by asking the students if they have ever entered an essay contest. Discuss responses. Ask students to explain what they would write about if the topic of a contest was "Conservation."

3. As you read the book, have students identify economic concepts and keep them in an economics journal. Have them focus on the situations in which the concepts occur.

4. Make a collage of **productive resources** (**natural, human, capital**). Find at least five of each. Identify each kind of resource by circling them with different colored markers.

5. Complete Handout 1. Discuss student responses.

6. Complete Handout 2. Let students show and explain their inventions.

7. **Optional:** Hold an Invention Fair. (See Follow-Up Activities below.)

Key Questions To Ask Students

1. What **good** was produced on Andy's farm? *(milk)* What important information did the farmers get each day on the radio? *(weather and prices)* Why do **prices** change? *(changes in **supply** and **demand**)*

2. Andy wants to **boycott** the contest. What is a boycott? *(refusing to buy, sell, or use a good or service in an attempt to influence policy)* Are boycotts legal? *(yes)*

3. How are the terms **productivity** and **conservation** similar? *(both deal with using resources efficiently)* Explain how Andy's bug idea was a way to increase productivity. *(get more food from the same amount of land)*

4. What do high **prices** tell us*? (Prices tell how scarce a good or service is relative to other goods and services.)* How can prices help us conserve? *(High prices encourage people to economize on the use of precious resources. They also provide an **incentive** — through higher profits — for producers to supply goods and services.)*

5. How do governments try to promote conservation? *(Governments set rules and regulations about resource use and pollution.)*

6. Who hired the health inspector? *(government)* Why? *(public safety)* Where did the money come from to pay the inspector? *(**taxes**)*

7. What are the three basic kinds of **taxes**? *(taxes on income, property, sales)* What are examples of each? *(income — federal, state, and local income tax, Social Security tax; property — taxes on land, inventory, houses; sales — excise tax, tax on purchases of goods and services)*

 Follow-Up Activities

1. *Essay Contest:* Have an economic theme for an essay contest.

2. *Conservation Decisions:* Create a journal based on daily "conservation decisions" students make.

3. *Invention Convention:* Conduct an invention convention. You could use the *Choices and Changes* curriculum (Intermediate Level) of the National Council on Economic Education. (www.ncee.net)

Prices Help Us Conserve!

Price is the clue that tells us how **scarce** a resource (or good or service) is compared to other resources. In general, the more scarce something is, the higher its price. When a valuable resource like oil becomes more scarce, its price rises. The high price does two things: 1. It encourages consumers to use less, often by switching to substitutes, and 2. It encourages producers to find and produce more oil since they want to make higher profits. This happens automatically in the oil markets without involving the government. Isn't this good news about conserving our natural resources?

On the back, answer these questions. Discuss your answers with your teacher.

1. What are some examples of **scarce natural resources**?
2. If we use lots of coal and it becomes more **scarce**, what will happen to its **price**?
3. What will **consumers** do as a result of this price change? Why?
4. What will **producers** of coal do as a result of this price change? Why?
5. How will these actions by consumers *and* producers influence the price of coal?

Draw a series of pictures illustrating these changes in the market for coal. Be creative. Below each picture, briefly explain what is happening.

Conservation Invention

Suppose you entered the Conservation Contest in the story. What invention would you come up with to help conserve valuable natural resources? Draw a picture below with a brief explanation.

List some of the **productive resources** you used to make the invention.

1. What do you think would be the **price** of the item you invented? _____

2. Do you think **businesses** would buy your invention? Why or why not? Would the **price** of your invention affect the decision of businesses to buy or not buy it?

3. If the **government** *made* businesses use your invention, how might this affect the prices of the products businesses sell? Do you think the government should do this? Why or why not?

Night of the Twister
By Ivy Ruckman

Summary

This story, based on a real event, tells how the Hatch family and the people of Grand Island, Nebraska, survive a night of terror when their town is devastated by several tornadoes. Together they not only live through the tragedy, but also rebuild their lives and their community. (Chapter book)

Key Economic Concepts

Productive Resources	Scarcity
Government Agencies	Taxes
Specialization	Public Goods

Materials

Handouts 1 and 2

 ## Teaching Procedure

1. Introduce the story by discussing storms and other natural disasters. Focus on the rebuilding that follows natural disasters.

2. Teach or review the economic concepts of **scarcity** and types of **productive resources**. Discuss the productive resources which are available before and after a tornado. Emphasize how many resources become relatively more scarce after a disaster. This is the reason that prices increase for generators, lanterns, bottled water, etc.

3. Read the story. Discuss key economic concepts as they appear. Have students keep a dictionary of these economic concepts. Another possibility is to have students keep a list of all the productive resources they find in the story on the Productive Resources handout in Part 3.

4. After reading the story, have the class create two lists of productive resources in the community before and after the storm. Have students write a paragraph comparing the two lists.

5. Complete Handout 1. Explain how government agencies, which are financed by **taxes**, are different from non-government agencies.

6. Complete Handout 2. Emphasize that government provides certain **public goods**, like road and national defense, since there are few incentives for private businesses to do so.

Key Questions To Ask Students

1. What government agencies or programs assisted the community after the twisters destroyed the town? *(Fire and Police, Civil Defense, National Guard, REACT, Government Housing, etc.)* How are government agencies supported? *(taxes)*

2. Why don't private businesses provide **public goods** like national defense and roads in a town? *(A private business wouldn't make a profit. It is virtually impossible to keep non-payers from using the roads or to get everyone to pay for national defense. Those who didn't pay would benefit anyway!)*

3. In this story, do you think that **human resources** (labor) and **natural resources** are of equal importance? Explain. *(Answers will vary.)*

4. Rebuilding a community takes much time and many scarce **productive resources**. How would you respond to someone who said, "I think that the tornado was ultimately good for the economy, since the rebuilding effort will provide employment for many workers." *(Wrong! The resources used to rebuild the community now cannot be used for other valuable uses in the economy. There really is an **opportunity cost**.)*

 Follow-Up Activities

1. *Bulletin Board:* Find newspaper articles regarding natural disasters and share these with the class. Make a bulletin board of these articles.

2. *Classroom Visitor:* Invite a police officer or other emergency officials to explain how they help during situations like tornadoes.

3. *Field Trip:* Take a field trip to the local Red Cross agency.

Handout 1

Community Services

1. In every community there are many services. What is the main difference between **government services** and **non-government services**?

2. List all the community services and organizations mentioned in the story. Put a circle around all those that are **government** services.

3. In the story, the police department and the Red Cross joined forces to help the community. List the ways these two agencies helped. Next, list ways they could have helped, but didn't.

....

Imagine your community has just been destroyed by a tornado. You are put in charge of creating an agency to assist the victims. Write a *plan of action*. In your plan include: types of services, funding sources, and any other significant information. How would you rebuild? What would you rebuild first? On another piece of paper, draw a diagram of your new community.

Government Services

1. What are examples of **government services** in your community? Where do government agencies get the money to operate?

2. What are examples of **non-government services** in your community? Where do these agencies get the money to operate?

3. Some services are provided by *both* governments and private businesses. Put an X in *one* of the three blanks to show how each service is provided.

	Government	Private Business	<u>Both</u> Government and Private Business
a. Fire Protection	_____	_____	_____
b. TV Repair	_____	_____	_____
c. Snow Removal	_____	_____	_____
d. 1st Class Mail	_____	_____	_____
e. National Defense	_____	_____	_____
f. Education	_____	_____	_____
g. Haircuts	_____	_____	_____
h. Mailing Packages	_____	_____	_____
i. Police Protection	_____	_____	_____
j. Trash Collection	_____	_____	_____
k. Street Cleaning	_____	_____	_____

4. Why are roads in your community something that <u>cannot</u> be provided very well by private business?

5. Which government service do you think is most important? Explain why.

Part 3

Handouts

To Use with Other Books

Decision Tree

Use the Decision Tree to help you make choices! Here are the steps:

1. Define the Problem
2. List the Two Choices
3. Evaluate the Choices (List good and bad points about each choice.)
4. Make a Decision!

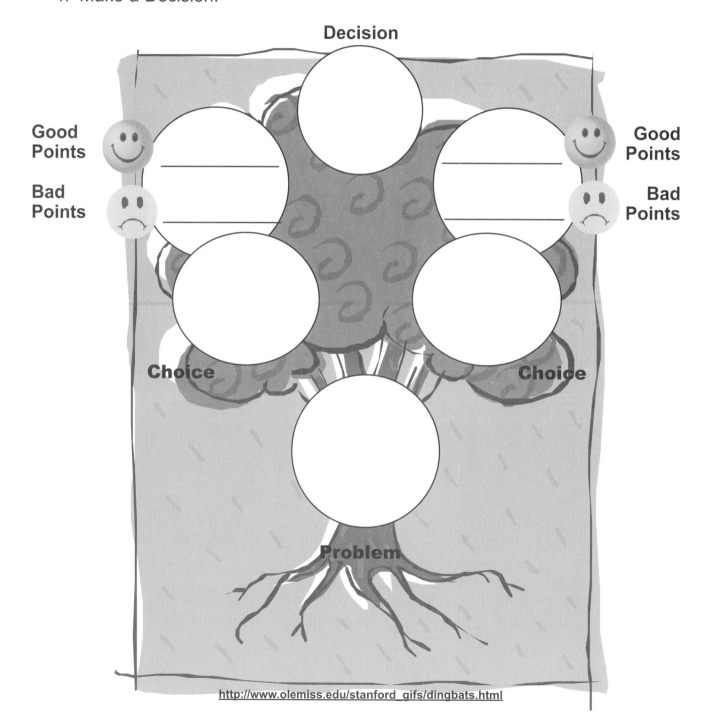

Five-Step Decision Model

Use the Five-Step Decision Model to help you make decisions!

1. **Define the Problem:** Analyze the situation; gather facts. What is the problem?

2. **List Alternative Solutions:** List feasible alternatives for solving the problem.

3. **List important criteria:** What important **values/goals** will influence the decision?

4. **Evaluate the Alternative Solutions:** Evaluate how each alternative "fits the criteria." Put +'s and –'s in grid to show if alternatives "fit" the criteria.

5. **Make a Decision!**

Decision Grid

	Criteria				
Alternatives					

Decisions, Decisions, Decisions!

The characters in many stories have to solve **scarcity** problems, and this usually means having to make some difficult decisions! Answer the questions below about a scarcity problem a book character had to solve.

1. What was a **scarcity problem** confronted by one of the book's characters?

   _____

2. What were the **alternatives** (choices) for solving the problem?

   _____

   _____

3. What **decision** did the character make?

   _____

4. What was the **opportunity cost** of the decision?

   _____

5. Write a paragraph explaining why you think it was a good or bad decision. Write neatly and use correct spelling and grammar.

My Scarcity Situations

People confront scarcity situations and scarcity problems every day. Answer the questions below about *your* scarcity situations.

a. Describe a **scarcity** situation you faced recently.

_____

_____

b. What was **scarce** in the situation? _____

c. What **decision** did you make? _____

_____

d. What was the **opportunity cost** of your decision? _____

_____

e. Write a paragraph about this or another scarcity situation. What decision did you make? Do you think you made a good decision? Explain why or why not.

Economics Is Everywhere!

Economics is everywhere! Give examples from the story, including page number, which illustrate the economic concepts below. (You may not find an example for every concept.) For longer books, complete the handout as you read.

Natural Resources:

Human Resources:

Capital Resources:

Scarcity:

Opportunity Cost:

Specialization:

Interdependence:

Exchange/Trade:

Role of Government in the Economy:

You will probably find other examples of economic concepts. List them on the back. (Other concepts include Profit, Economic Systems, Supply, Demand, Entrepreneurship, International Trade, and Competition. You may find even more concepts!)

Productive Resources

In almost all stories there are examples of many types of productive resources.
In the book you just read, identify some of them.

Natural Resources (or Raw Materials)	Human Resources	Capital Resources

In the space below, draw the **Production Model** showing the productive resources being combined to produce a good or service.

Interdependence Web

In an economy, people and businesses **specialize** in what they produce. They then must **depend** upon each other to provide productive resources, goods, and services. In the center of the "Interdependence Web" below, put a character in the story who had to depend upon others. In the other circles, put the people (businesses, workers, etc.) the character depended on.

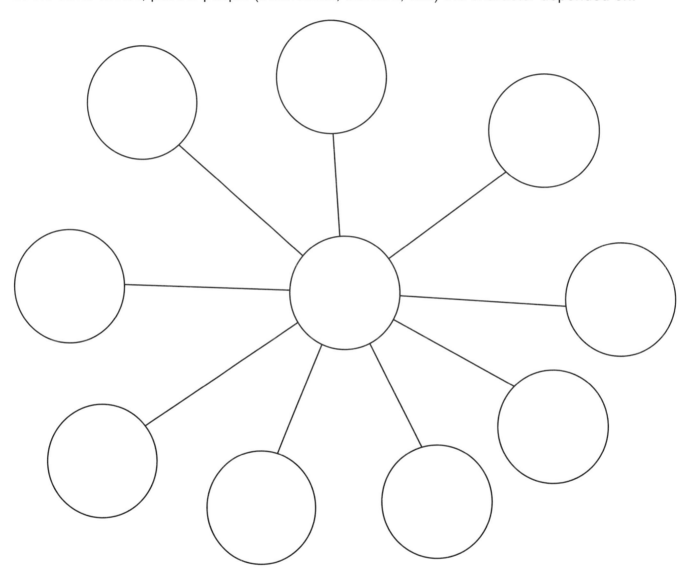

In the story did it help when the character depended on others? _____ Explain below.

On the back write a paragraph explaining your answer.

What's in a Job?

Many different kinds of **human resources** are needed to produce goods and services. Pick a job done by a character in the story you just read, then answer the questions.

What is the character's job? _____

What special skills (**human capital**) does the character need to do the job?

What education or training do you think is necessary for this job?

What are the good points and bad points about the job?

Good Points:

Bad Points:

What good or service do <u>you</u> want to produce when you grow up?

Write a paragraph entitled, "What I Want to Produce When I Grow Up."

Trading Around the World

In many stories you learn about people from all over the world. Our economy depends upon the productive resources, goods, and services that we get by trading with other countries.

Each person should search the classroom (or home) for clothing and items produced in other countries. Write them down on scrap paper. Then meet in small groups and list at least ten items, each from a <u>different</u> country. Mark these on a wall map or on a transparency of the world. What patterns do you see?

ITEM	COUNTRY
_____	_____
_____	_____
_____	_____
_____	_____
_____	_____
_____	_____
_____	_____
_____	_____
_____	_____
_____	_____

On the back write a paragraph explaining how trading helps countries.

Economics Bingo!

There are many economic words and ideas in the stories you have read. After reading the stories and learning about economics, you are now ready to play the Economics Bingo Game!

First, write BINGO in the shaded squares. Your teacher will list all the economics words you have studied on the board. On the Bingo card write one of these words in each square. (You may write a word only once under each letter.) Your teacher will draw these words "out of a hat" and say the definition. Put a token on the square if you have the word. Five in a row makes Economics Bingo! (For an "already-made" Econ Bingo game see www.kidseconposters.com.)

		Free Space		

Three Cheers for Capital Resources!

1. Give three examples of **capital resources** in the story you read.

2. Explain how each capital resource increased **productivity**.

3. How do businesses <u>get</u> capital resources?

- -

A Capital Invention!

In the space below, draw a **capital resource** that you invented to help produce a special good or solve a special problem. Below your drawing, explain how the capital resource works. Report to the class.

'Round and 'Round the Economy Goes!

Use people, businesses, goods and services, and productive resources from the story to fill in/label the **Circular Flow Model** of the economy. Also, show which way the money flows.

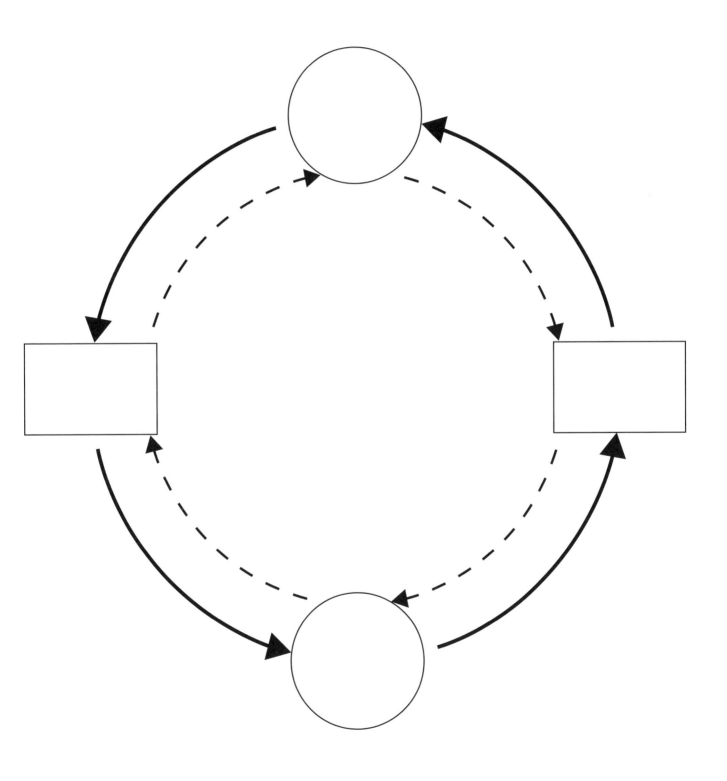

Part 4

Econ Book Report

To Use with Other Children's Literature Books

"Econ" Book Report

Name _____

Book Title _____

Author _____

Illustrator _____

Number of Pages _____   Fiction _____   Non Fiction _____

Setting _____

Main Characters _____

_____

_____

What happens at the end of the story?

_____

_____

_____

_____

Draw a picture and/or explain the economic concepts you found in this story. If you can't find an example, write "NONE" in the box. On the back, draw boxes showing other economic concepts you found in the story.

Good	Service	Scarcity

Specialization	Interdependence	Opportunity Cost

Human Resource	Capital Resource	Price

On a scale of 1 to 5, with "5" being the very best, I give this book a:

1   2   3   4   5

Part 5

Literature Connection

Other Books You Can Use To Teach Economics

Literature Connection

Other Books You Can Use
To Teach Economics

The books listed below are excellent for teaching economic content to students. At first glance, the books may not seem to have an economic connection. However, economics is so pervasive in our world that these books — and virtually any book — can easily be used to teach some economic content.

Teachers will be pleased to discover that short lessons on each book can be found at the popular **KidsEcon Posters**© web site. (See www.kidseconposters.com. Click on **Literature Connection**.) Each lesson provides key questions to ask students that focus on the economic content.

Goods and Services

> *Jennie's Hat* — Erza Jack Keats
> *Katy and the Big Snow* — Virginia Lee Burton
> *My New York* — Kathy Jacobsen
> *My Town* — William Wegman
> *Pigs Go to Market* — Amy Axelrod
> *Rumpelstiltskin's Daughter* — Diane Stanley
> *To Market, To Market* — Anne Miranda
> *Too Many Chickens* — Paulette Bourgeois
> *Trashy Town* — Andrea Zimmerman
> *Who Wants a Cheap Rhinoceros?* — Shel Silverstein

Economic Wants

> *Bear Wants More* — Karma Wilson
> *Click Clack Moo: Cows That Type* — Doreen Cronin
> *How Much Is That Doggie in the Window?* — Bob Merrill
> *If You Give a Pig a Pancake* — Laura Numeroff
> *Just Shopping With Mom* — Mercer Mayer

Producers

> *Apple Farmer Annie* — Monica Wellington
> *Earning Money* — Natalie M. Rosinsky
> *Farming (America at Work series)* — Ann Love & Jane Drake
> *The Hatseller and the Monkey* — Baba Wague Diakite
> *The Little Red Hen Makes a Pizza* — Philemon Sturges
> *The Popcorn Book* — Tomie dePaola
> *Sweet Potato Pie* — Kathleen D. Lindsey

Consumers

Benny's Pennies — Pat Brisson
The Big Buck Adventure — Shelly Gill & Deborah Tobola
The Ox-Cart Man — Donald Hall
Something Special for Me — Vera B. Williams
Spending Money — Natalie M. Rosinsky

Productive Resources

Apples — Gail Gibbons
Extra Cheese, Please! — Chris Peterson
The Goat in the Rug — Charles L. Blood
How To Make an Apple Pie and See the World — Margorie Priceman
Milk From Cow to Carton — Aliki Brandenberg
The Life and Times of the Peanut — Charles Micucci
Pancakes, Pancakes — Eric Carle
The Pot That Juan Built — Nancy Andrews-Goebel
The Tortilla Factory — Gary Paulsen

Natural Resources

Agatha's Feather Bed — Carmen Agra Deedy
Forestry (America at Work series) — Jane Drake and Ann Love
The Giving Tree — Shel Silverstein
Growing Vegetable Soup — Lois Ehlert
Just a Dream — Chris Van Allsburg

Human Resources

Abuela's Weave — Omar Castenada
Charlie Needs a Cloak — Tomie dePaola
How a Book Is Made — Aliki Brandenberg
How Santa Got His Job — S. Krensky
Walter the Baker — Eric Carle
Working Cotton — Sheryl Ann Williams

Capital Resources

Apples for Life — Alan Zepeda
Mining (America at Work series) — Jane Drake and Ann Love
The Three Little Wolves and the Big Bad Pig — Eugene Trivizas
Tools — Ann Morris

Scarcity

Bringing the Rain to Kapiti Plain — Verna Aardema
Budgeting (How Economics Works series) — Sandy Donovan
The Doorbell Rang — Pat Hutchins
Getting' Through Thursday — Melrose Cooper
The Lorax — Dr. Seuss
One Grain of Rice — Demi
Reuben and the Quilt — Merle Good
Sam and the Lucky Money — Karen Chinn

Opportunity Cost

Erandi's Braids — Antonio Hernandez Madrigal
Mailing May — Michael O'Tunnell
Tops & Bottoms — Janet Stevens

Trade and Money

Bearhide and Crow — Paul Brett Johnson
Bunny Money — Rosemary Wells
Cash, Credit Cards, or Checks: A Book about Payment Methods
    — Nancy Loewen
From Beads to Banknotes: The Story of Money — Neale S.
    Godfrey
The Go-Around Dollar — Barbara Johnston Adams
A New Coat for Anna — Harriet Ziefert
Once Upon a Dime — Nancy Kelly Allen
Pig and Crow — Kay Chorao
Pigs Will Be Pigs — Amy Axelrod
Round and Round the Money Goes — Melvin & Gilda Berger
Saturday Sancocho — Leyla Torres
Why Money Was Invented — Neale S. Godfrey

Specialization

How a House is Built — Gail Gibbons
My Dad's Job — Peter Glassman
Thank You, Mr. Falker — Patricia Polacco
Tony's Bread — Tomie dePaola
Worms Gets a Job — Kathy Caple

Interdependence

Grandpa's Corner Store — Dyanne DiSalvo-Ryan
The World in a Supermarket — Adjoa J. Burrowes

Trade-Offs

Letting Swift River Go — Jane Yolen

Productivity

Curious George Goes to a Chocolate Factory — H. A. Rey
The Furry News: How To Make a Newspaper — Loreen Leedy

Market

Saturday Market — Patricia Grossman & Enrique O. Sanchez
The Stock Market **(How Economics Works series)** — Donna Jo Fuller
Stock Market Pie — J.M. Seymour
Stock Market Smart — McGowan Dumas
Ups and Downs: A Book About the Stock Market — Nancy Loewen

Price

The Big Buck Adventure — Shelley Gill & Deborah Tobola
A Dollar for Penny — Dr. Julie Glass
Estela's Swap — Alexis O'Neill
Leah's Pony — Elizabeth Friedrich
The Penny Pot — Stuart Murphy
Sold! — Nathan Zimelman

Supply and Demand

Arthur's TV Trouble — Marc Brown
Lemonade for Sale — Stuart J. Murphy
Dan's Pants: The Adventures of Dan, The Fabric Man —
    Merle Good with Dan & Fran Boltz
Paperboy — Mary K Kroeger & Louise Borden

Entrepreneur

An **ENTREPRENEUR** is someone who takes the risk to develop a new product or start a new business.

Entrepreneurs hope many consumers will buy their products so they can earn profits.

Example: Henry Ford was a successful entrepreneur who risked his personal savings to produce automobiles that people could afford to buy.

Better Than a Lemonade **Stand** — Daryl Berstein
Earning Money **(How Economics Works series)** — Patricia J. Murphy
The Kid's Business Book — Arlene Erlbach
Little Nino's Pizzeria — Karen Barbour
Look Lake Fishing Derby — K. Cook Waldron
Vision of Beauty — Kathryn Lasky
What's the Big Idea, Ben Franklin? — Jean Fritz

Profit

PROFIT is the difference between the money people make when they produce and sell a good or service and all their costs of production.

Example: Sharon sells a glass of lemonade for 50¢. If all her costs of production are 21¢, then she will earn a profit of 29¢ on each glass she sells.

Arthur's Pet Business — Marc Brown
How the Second Grade Got $8,205.50 To Visit the Statue of Liberty — Nathan Zimelman

Savings

SAVING is the part of a person's income that is *not* spent for goods and services or used to pay taxes.

People can earn INTEREST on the money they save.

Example: Jerome is saving $5.00 per week at his local bank. His goal is to purchase a bicycle. Jerome knows that the money he puts in a savings account earns INTEREST.

Alexander, Who Used to Be Rich Last Sunday — Judith Viorst
The Babe and I — David A. Adler
Banking **(How Economics Works series)** — Barbara Allman
A Chair for My Mother — Vera B. Williams
Check It Out: The Book About Banking — Neale S. Godfrey
Saving Money **(How Economics Works series)** — Philip Heckman
Spend, Save, or Donate?: A Book About Managing Money — Nancy Loewen
Uncle Jed's Barbershop — M. King Mitchell

Investing

INVESTING occurs when people and businesses use money to purchase capital goods or increase the skills and abilities of workers.

People and businesses invest so they can increase PRODUCTIVITY.

Example: Rami will use his savings to purchase a better mower for his lawn-mowing business. Now he will be able to mow more lawns and earn more money.

Captain Abdul's Pirate School — Colin McNaughton
A Money Adventure — Neale S. Godfrey
My Rows and Piles of Coins — Tololwa M. Mollel